The Love of Anxiety

AND OTHER ESSAYS

Books by Charles Frankel

✡

THE LOVE OF ANXIETY AND OTHER ESSAYS

THE FAITH OF REASON

THE CASE FOR MODERN MAN

THE DEMOCRATIC PROSPECT

Books Edited by Charles Frankel

✡

ROUSSEAU'S SOCIAL CONTRACT

THE USES OF PHILOSOPHY: AN IRWIN EDMAN READER

ISSUES IN UNVERSITY EDUCATION

THE GOLDEN AGE OF AMERICAN PHILOSOPHY

The Love of Anxiety

AND OTHER ESSAYS

BY CHARLES FRANKEL

Harper & Row, Publishers

New York, Evanston, and London

FIRST EDITION

LIBRARY OF CONGRESS CATALOG CARD NUMBER: 65-14652

D-P

To Susan

Contents

Foreword

THE ESSAYS AND THE FABLE THAT HAVE BEEN GATHERED TO-
gether in this book were written at different times and in different moods. Some were composed, for stately occasions, on
subjects proposed to me; others were written with no provocation at all, and I am just as surprised as the next man to see
what their subject turned out to be. I have written on some
themes because they troubled me, on others because they gave
me pleasure. And I have written on a broad variety of subjects
because that is the pleasure of being a philosopher.

Yet a central theme is present in nearly all the pieces. That
theme is one of the more curious phenomena of our time—the
love of anxiety. All unprejudiced observers of the human scene
have for long recognized that man has a spontaneous inclina-
tion to prefer pain to pleasure. Philosophical hedonists, who are
usually grim and unsmiling sorts, exemplify this truth. They
think that man *ought* to prefer pleasure to pain, thereby making the pursuit of pleasure a matter of principle and taking all
the pleasure out of it. But the love of anxiety, though it is an
enduring human amusement, has today become more than
this. It has become a social outlook, a philosophical preoccupation, and something very close to a way of life.

Sean O'Casey speaks somewhere of "somber messages, hailed
as profound meditations, incontrovertible, showing life buttoned up in everlasting woe." These messages have now ac-

quired a strength, an audience, and a solemn intellectual prestige that make them a significant social phenomenon. What lies behind this cultivated love of anxiety? Clearly, in its own way, it offers a kind of consolation. It is neither sentimental nor callous, it shows deep concern about the human situation, and it connects the troubles that disturb us every day to the ultimate disjointedness of the universe. The process is a little like treating a toothache by inducing a fever throughout the body. The pain is dulled by the surrounding sense of general unease.

But there is something more than a desire to assuage our pain behind the love of anxiety. There are also some intellectual reasons, some very well-established habits of mind that have had a long career and an honorable reputation in our civilization. One of these is the belief that methods of rational inquiry are quite inappropriate outside the rather limited realm of physical objects for which they are intended, and that other methods than reason should be used where human affairs and human problems are concerned. In the essay "The Anti-Intellectualism of the Intellectuals" and in the title essay I examine the merits of this point of view.

Two other intellectual attitudes seem to me also to have much to do with the love of anxiety. The first is the tendency to employ moral and social ideals that are themselves left unexamined as standards for the criticism of modern thought and modern society. Such ideals often rest on notions of human capacity that are unrealistic, and take little account of the limited historical options that are actually available to us. The natural consequence, when social and moral criticism is conducted in this way, is the helpless feeling that we are in the grip of some sort of cosmic conspiracy. And yet, when such ideals are brought out into the open, and seriously considered as proposals for the organization of human life, they turn out, as often as not, to be intrinsically unattractive. The tendency to conduct moral and social criticism from the vantage point of ideals that are not themselves regarded as fair game for analysis is well entrenched in intellectual tradition and is a characteristic of liberals and conservatives both. It is one of the reasons why intellectuals have contributed less to the guidance of their societies than they might otherwise have done.

The second intellectual habit which feeds the love of anxiety consists in the treatment of social problems as though they could be reduced to matters of individual psychology. But most social problems are the collective consequence of unnumbered human actions playing back and forth on one another. Where such questions are concerned, attention to the social framework that creates these unintended consequences is decisive. The reform of the human psyche is not enough, and in many cases is entirely irrelevant. In any case, human traits like envy, vanity, and plain, straightforward malice are probably with us to stay. The question to ask of social institutions is how they control and orient human drives and emotions; it is not whether they provide spiritual redemption. When we think in terms of spiritual redemption, either we leave ourselves permanently alienated from the world of politics and social action, or else we lose ourselves in angry forms of utopianism. Unfortunately, a large part of the history of the intellectual in modern politics is described in this sentence. It should not be surprising, if this is true, that anxiety should be in intellectual fashion.

But this is a statement of principles, and I had better stop. I shall mislead the reader if I go on. For what interests me more than my principles is what escapes my principles. The tension between generalities and specifics, between principles and practice, is much more entertaining and instructive where morals and politics are concerned than any set of pure abstractions can be. And not everything in this book has to do either with principles or with problems, or even with anxiety. In the end, I wrote these essays simply because I really couldn't think of anything better to do with my time. It would be very gratifying if the reader, in the time he spends with them, felt the same way.

The Love of Anxiety

I

Existentialism, or Cosmic Hypochondria

NOT ALL INTELLECTUALS THESE DAYS HAVE TURNED OFFICIALLY "religious"; but religious preoccupations, a concern with the presence or absence of a transcendent Meaning or Design in the universe, have become respectable. It has become a little *déclassé*, a symptom of shallowness and of not having arrived at a man's estate, to fail to take the supernatural seriously, whether or not you believe in it.

This is true even for the atheist. The atheism of Jean-Paul Sartre, to take the most prominent example, is a disabused, transcendental atheism. Its humanism and naturalism are tinged with nostalgia for the supernatural. It sees man as a fallen angel, a creature wishing for perfection and wholeness of spirit but condemned to half-truths and bad faith, and forever caught between two worlds in neither of which he can be at home. And it sees the universe, now that "God is dead," as a formless something-that-is-nothing, in which man bumptiously and absurdly decides that life is going to have a meaning anyway. In short, this atheism sees man and his place in nature much as the traditional religions of the West say you must see them if you do not believe in God. It rejects religion, but it gives expression to religion's transcendental perspectives and transcendental dilemmas.

There has been since the war, in short, the resurgence of a kind of attitude to which religion has traditionally played host, and out of which new creeds and moralities have frequently emerged. Religious and philosophical literature has expressed a revolt against the things which displaced the religious emotions in the period between the two world wars—the utopian hopes that went into Communism, the deification of the State and the Leader by Fascism, the lesser cults of technology and engineering and better business which drew to themselves a kind of devotion that had previously been reserved for ideals beyond this world. These things have seemed to religious minds, and to many disenchanted worldlings as well, to be not simply instances of false hopes and corrupted standards, but the natural consequences of "secularism," of the attempt to base human ideals and human institutions on purely human needs and worldly concerns.

These struggles with secular gods and with rational substitutes for faith account in large part for what has become the characteristic emphasis of current religious literature on the "transcendence" of God, as well as the characteristic emphasis of much current philosophical literature on the limits of reason. And to express these twin attitudes in terms of an inclusive set of beliefs about man and the world there has been at hand a remarkably apt and flexible intellectual tradition—existentialism. The theme of existentialism is the great theme of Hegel—the itinerary of the mind through life and time. It is interested, as Hegel was, not so much in the abstract logic of reason as in the drama of its development—its beginning, middle, and end, its fortunes and misfortunes, its tragic blindnesses and comic impertinences, and its climactic recognition scenes in which it comes to self-consciousness about its conditions and destiny. But existentialism fundamentally alters the meaning of this drama. For the great recognition scenes in Hegel are those in which one discovers that all is rational, that history and existence are the enactments of an inexorable Reason, and the individual life the playing out of a predetermined role. But the great recognition scenes in existentialism are those in which one discovers that mind and reason are the creatures of existence, provoked by its practical demands, hemmed in by its irrational urgencies, limited to its temporal horizons. Existentialism is brokenhearted Hegelianism—an encounter not with Reason but with Absurdity.

Existentialism is part of that large tidal drift of ideas in the modern world, in which such otherwise divergent philosophies as Marxism and John Dewey's instrumentalism are also caught up, which have emphasized "the existential determination of thought" and have rejected the classic notion of mind as a pure and disembodied thing. All these philosophies have had to rethink seriously what might be meant by such fundamental intellectual and moral ideals as "objectivity" and "truth." But where philosophic Marxism and instrumentalism, each in its own quite different way, have continued to believe that objectivity and truth are meaningful and attainable ideals, existentialism has given up the ghost. Man, as the existentialist sees him, cannot help but measure all he thinks and does in terms of these transcendent ideals; yet he can neither define them nor attain them. And this, in the end, is the nature of "the human situation": man is doomed to strive, to seek, and not to find—and yet he must not yield.

The center of the existentialist vision lies here. It is, as it were, a systematic way of seeing things in double focus—man's generalizations against his innate partisanship, man's desire to communicate with others against his inalienable isolation within himself, man's search for the limitless and the absolute against the limitations and the relativity of everything he thinks and does. It is a vision which makes all thought and all practice incurably subjective. Loneliness, despair, and anxiety become not merely passing moods but instances of the deepest form of awareness. And crisis and tension become not specific problems to be overcome by specific techniques but the ineluctable features of "the existential situation." The Crucifixion, as Kierkegaard, the father of existentialism, observed, is the symbol of human life; "the foolishness of the Cross" becomes all the fulfillment of which life is capable in its own terms.

There have been, by and large, three ways of living with this vision. The first has been to say, with Sartre and the atheistic existentialists, that "man is condemned to be free," that he must leap in the dark and commit himself to transcendent ideals despite their absurdity and his own impotence. The second is to stress, with Simone Weil, the divergent poles of "Gravity" and "Grace," and to turn, with Catholic existentialists like Gabriel Marcel, to the saving power of the supernatural. The third is to convert the duality of the existentialist view into what Tillich calls "the Protestant principle"—the recognition of the presence, behind all human affirmations and ideals, of the "Unconditioned."

We have had in this century enough of idolatry and utopian hopes, of egoism masked as altruism, and of altruism that has been only a form of moral imperialism to understand the force and point of these ideas. Anxiety, the impotent fear of some nameless doom, has become an institutionalized way of life. The emotional context of existentialist philosophy and religion is the same as that of the most characteristic contemporary fiction and poetry. We may read the books of J. D. Salinger on one level and think that he is talking about the loneliness and disorientation of adolescents; but what gives his work its appeal to adolescents and to others is that he is writing about adult as well as youthful ways of losing and finding one's way, and about the supernatural as well as the natural landscape on which we are lost. It is symbolic, and not, perhaps, entirely an accident, that so many of the leading figures in the present movement in religious thought—Simone Weil and Nicholas Berdyaev, Paul Tillich and Martin Buber—have been actual exiles.

In short, existentialism, like the great classic philosophies and religions, has given a meaning to the experience of its time by making the most conspicuous features of that experience seem also to be the necessary features of the universe as a whole. We have had to live through an era of mass irrationality which has made liberal hopes seem, to say the least, premature; existentialism tells us that unreason is a cardinal feature of the universe. We have had to witness cruelty of unimaginable, and seemingly purposeless, scope and horror; existentialism tells us that Sin and Evil are radical facts of life. In its own strange way, existentialism brings consolation, by telling us that our pains are not avoidable, and that our anguish is the anguish of all existence.

Yet, in considering existentialism, it is important to keep two questions apart which are often confused. The first is the reason for existentialism's widespread appeal. The second is the question whether it is true. With respect to this second question, a brief illustration may help suggest the kind of argument on which existentialism depends. "Existents appear," Sartre says in

Being and Nothingness, "they are encountered, but they can never be inferentially deduced. . . . There is not the least reason for our 'being-there.' " Accordingly, in Sartre's view, every existing thing is *"de trop,"* "superfluous," "absurd." But is it not really a rather simple error to move from the impossibility of showing by logical demonstration that the world as it is could not possibly be otherwise (that is, that no existent can be "inferentially deduced") to the wildly irrelevant implication that "there is not the least reason," no way of explaining, why it is as it is? It is not logically necessary that human beings should have thirty-two teeth; they might have had thirty-six or twenty-eight. But does this mean that teeth are "superfluous" or that thirty-two is an "absurd" number of teeth to have? "Things have become too easy," Kierkegaard once wrote. "It is time to make them difficult again." Perhaps so; but things have been getting difficult enough by themselves without getting help from the philosophers.

What is significant about such arguments is not simply the abuse of logic and common sense which they involve, but the fact that they lead directly to the inverting of what until now have been commonly accepted intellectual standards. Paradox and mystery become the conclusions of inquiry rather than its beginning; moral courage and philosophical wisdom come to be indistinguishable; and anxiety and the fear of death are recommended as cures for old philosophical errors and as preludes to the discovery of philosophic truth. Existentialism is not the first philosophy to exemplify Fichte's maxim, "We philosophize out of the need for redemption." But it goes further than any other philosophy in recent memory in affirming that whatever redeems us is true.

Yet it is these very consequences which explain existentialism's appeal. Despite its confusing dialectic—perhaps because of it—existentialism speaks directly and intimately to men who feel lonely and helpless before the play of events. To speak of "the absurdity of existence," to refer to the "inanity of things," are ways of expressing the facelessness of a mass culture which, for so many, has submerged personal relations and made individual achievement seem meaningless and *"de trop."* Nor is it hard to understand why brave and sensitive men in the French Resistance, fighting against Nazi infamy, should have asked themselves, even while fighting, what in the world they could possibly be fighting for. The restoration of the tired, purposeless politics of the French Third Republic could hardly have been a compelling reason. Yet there was no strong reason to hope that they were really fighting for anything better. Why should they have done what they did except that a man must simply say "No" at times, whether or not he has any positive reason or faith to support him? Existentialism reminds us that in our world the simplest and humblest decencies have for long periods of time been impossible to practice and not entirely possible to believe in even abstractly. It represents the effort, in an age of fanaticism and of mass movements, to find a last-ditch defense for integrity, and for the freedom and distinctiveness of the individual.

Moreover, existentialism, particularly in its French form, has represented an assault on the modern intellectual's twin temptations—the temptation to apply a cruelly intellectualist system of thought to the cloudy and compromised world of political actuality, and the temptation to withdraw entirely from that world. Existentialism has attacked these temptations at their intellectual source—the Cartesian ideal of rationality, of clear, distinct, and indubitable principles based on clear, distinct, and indubitable premises. Existentialism has tried to establish a new standard of rationality for the guidance of human beings, one less likely to entangle them in cold abstractions and perfection-ist formulas, one more capable of permitting men of principle to take definite sides in the ambiguous and morally indefinite struggles of their time without loss of intellectual honesty or self-respect.

Gabriel Marcel does not write plays simply to present his philosophical principles in forceful dramatic form. He writes them because they are intrinsic to what he wants to say—that abstractions and formulas, essences and principles, are the masks of equivocal human passions, and express personal, not imper-sonal, commitments. Nor is it an accident that Sartre also writes novels and plays, or that Camus (who disliked, with some rea-son, to call himself an "existentialist") moved back and forth from expository essays to philosophical novels in which ex-plicit abstractions are firmly suppressed. The critique of the Cartesian ideal of rationality represents existentialism's major contribution to the reorientation of French and of Western moral attitudes and intellectual culture.

But it may be wondered, from a strictly philosophical point of view, whether the assault had to go so far, or be quite so theatrical in its tone. For all their poignancy and pertinence, existentialism and the religious and antireligious philosophies it has nurtured are not quite to the logical point. The consolation they bring involves precisely that confusion of "the relative" with "the absolute" which these philosophies claim is the source of all error and bad faith. Existentialism, as its spokesmen say, is an "encounter with nothingness," a battle to overcome modern nihilism. But nihilism as it is experienced—the actual "existential" sense of the meaninglessness and futility of life—is not the product of an intellectual theory, and it does not take a new theology or metaphysics to overcome it. It is the product of broken hopes, lost friends, impermanent commitments, and declining standards; and it may even be the symptom of a loss of intestinal fortitude.

There is a simpler sort of ministry than that envisaged in existentialism—the care of widows and orphans, the practice of charity, the cultivation of love. The existentialists, it need hardly be said, do not oppose this sort of ministry. But they bury it under words like "absurdity," whose meaning has been torn out of context. Their argument that moral ideals are "leaps in the dark," assertions of principles in a world that is resistant to principles, has nothing logically to do with the conditions and consequences that men must take into account, and the actual criteria that men use, when they are trying, soberly and responsibly, to decide how to act and where to stand in the world of practice. It is a verbal argument, which proves only the impossibility of attaining demonstrative certainty in human affairs, and which borrows its force from that Cartesian pattern of mind which existentialism presumably wishes to reject.

In brief, existentialism is a reflection of our troubles, and not an answer to them. And it is a reflection of our troubles in a slightly cracked mirror. For existentialism has elevated experiences which all of us have occasionally into the permanent and decisive qualities of life. The existentialist stress upon the necessity to be committed, to be "engaged," is, after all, a slight redundancy for most of us, who, even in this age of alleged catastrophe, are already engaged as lovers, parents, jobholders, and citizens. To make such a point of "engagement" in the abstract bespeaks a very special kind of isolation. Despite all its associations with the characteristic moods of a postwar world, one cannot help but feel that existentialism lacks balance and catholicity, and that, in the end, it is the metaphysics of the emotionally unemployed.

The absurdity which existentialism finds, and comes close to celebrating, is not the absurdity of existence. It is the absurdity of the ideals in terms of which this philosophy measures the human scene. Other philosophies, quite different from existentialism in their spirit, also stress that all human beliefs are fallible and all human ideals corrigible. To make this assertion, it is not necessary to cling to transcendental passions or to announce that since such passions cannot be satisfied all human ideals are at bottom absurd. It may not be that existentialism holds that all human ideals are on the same level. One imagines, for example, that Professor Tillich intends his "Protestant principle" to be more than a principle of protest against all ideals. But it is difficult to see what more it is. For it is simply a comprehensive principle, asserting that, no matter what ideal you affirm or espouse, it is not all that can be affirmed or espoused. But it is theatrics, not wisdom, to make such an absolute principle out of protest, and then to give as one's reason the inane argument that nothing is perfect, that everything has its taint of mortality. This turns normal, useful, everyday skepticism into an operatic posture.

A philosophy which offers nothing more than this, which offers no relevant principles in terms of which we can distinguish the better ideal from the worse, imperfect though all ideals may be, seems a less than adequate basis for religion or philosophy, and for politics and morality. As an expression of the distracted modern spirit, or as a form of shock treatment for the complacent, existentialism has unquestionable merits. But terror produces its own form of inertia, and is not an attractive antidote to complacency. And cosmic hypochrondria is not, it seems to me, a sound basis on which to build a modern philosophy, a modern religion, or a clear and candid mind.

II

---◆---

The Anti-Intellectualism of the Intellectuals

"It was intelligence," kierkegaard wrote in his *Journals,* "it was intelligence and nothing else that had to be opposed. Presumably this is why I, who had the job, was armed with an immense intelligence." Other immense intelligences also have devoted their lives to opposing intelligence; the assault on reason is a major part of the Western intellectual tradition. In a quite neutral and exactly descriptive sense of the phrase, there is an anti-intellectualism of the intellectuals.

It is not the anti-intellectualism of the mob or the Philistine. It does not aim to put intellectuals in their place or to pen up intelligence within the cage of safe, sane, down-to-earth interests. It respects speculation, detachment, the impractical, the unconventional. But it is anti-intellectualism just the same. For it lays down its own rules for speculation; it has its own definitions of detachment and impracticality, and its own conventions about what is unconventional. And these rules, definitions, and conventions, I believe, are incompatible with the conduct of the intellectual life in a disciplined and responsible manner.

Moreover, for all its intramural character as a doctrine of, by, and for intellectuals, this proudly articulate distrust of reason has larger political and social consequences. Over the past two hundred years, there have been repeated outbreaks of impatience with intellectual freedom, repeated attacks on intellectuals for their excessive innocence or their excessive sophistication, for their hunger for power or their retreat to the ivory tower. And for every one of these vulgar assaults on the life of the mind one can find a refined and highly intellectualized doctrine which is its counterpart. Underneath the anti-intellectualism of the market place and the street corner there has been a continuous stream of ideas expressing the alienation of intellectuals themselves from the intellectual life. And this anti-intellectualism of the café and the academy has given status and a voice to its cousin from the bush.

I do not mean to hold philosophers like Kierkegaard or novelists like D. H. Lawrence guilty by association of anti-intellectualism. It is absurd to say of a mind like Pascal's that it was hostile to intelligence because it distinguished between reasons of the heart and reasons of the head and gave so much credence to the former. Such views must be examined on their merits, however much they may resemble or encourage more vulgar views. In any case, they cannot be blamed for the existence of anti-intellectualism, which would exist without their help; it is part of the old Adam in man.[1] But since it is part of the old

[1] Richard Hofstadter, in his distinguished study, *Anti-intellectualism in American Life* (New York: Alfred A. Knopf, 1964), prefers to call the intellectual doctrines I have in mind "antirationalism," wishing to separate them sharply from the more brutal forms of anti-intellectualism. This is a matter of labels, and he is right, of course, that Hemingway's anti-intellectualism is not the same as Joe McCarthy's, and Nietzsche's not the same as Hitler's. They differ in intellectual quality and interest, and in their intentions. Yet Professor Hofstadter inculpates John Dewey not simply in the history of antirationalism but in the history of American popular anti-intellectualism, holding that Dewey gave expression to ideas, attitudes, and unresolved problems in our culture whose "tendency and consequences" are anti-intellectual. If this can be said with even an appearance of plausibility about Dewey, who spent so

Adam in man, it is fair and necessary to speak of an anti-intellectualism of the intellectuals. Intellectuals are, after all, part of the human race. However civilized their conscious intentions may be, and however loyal they may be to the rights and privileges of their fellow members of "the scribbling set," they are susceptible to the same emotions other people are, including impatience and weariness with the intellectual life, and animal fear of its consequences. And their doctrines feed these emotions, whether that is their conscious purpose or not.

Mind, says Professor Norman Brown, a contemporary and eloquent spokesman for this proudly articulate anti-intellectualism, is at the end of its tether. It has been exposed, in the mad world it has made, as the kind of madness it is. We now know that science, the scholarship practiced in the universities, and orderly discursive thought in general are merely the conventional tools of conventional fools, forms of madness that seem sane only because they are the standard operating madnesses of the world. But there is another, divinely touched madness that transcends these. "Our real choice is between holy and unholy madness: open your eyes and look around you—madness is in the saddle anyhow. . . . Resisting madness can be the maddest way of being mad."[2] No doubt these sentiments do not express the same dull, brutal hatred of intellect that infected Nazism. Still, a call to a higher form of madness can hardly be called a defense of the life of reason. And it stands at the end of a long tradition

much of his life defining and defending the logic of rational inquiry, how much more strongly can it be said of Hemingway or Nietzsche? Nomenclature is often a matter of emphasis. I would prefer to speak of an anti-intellectualism of the intellectuals because I think that the "tendency and consequences" of much that intellectuals have said is to cast doubt not simply on rational inquiry but even on orderly discourse and intelligent self-control.

2 "Apocalypse," *Harper's Magazine*, May, 1961.

which has held that reason is a form of madness, an unholy form, and has argued that there are other and better ways to discover the truth of things.

Rousseau put more faith in his "feeling heart." Wordsworth spoke of a "wise passiveness," which is preferable to the intellectual analysis that "murders to dissect." Nietzsche thought reason the poor man's substitute for insight, the weak man's vengeance against the truly free spirit. D. H. Lawrence, Henri Bergson, Georges Sorel, William James, and Jean-Paul Sartre has each in his own way cast doubts on the competence of human intelligence and the authenticity of rational ideals. The anti-intellectualism of the intellectuals is a powerful tradition, and many of the most legitimately honored intelligences in our history have contributed to it. And for all we know, it may be justified.

In any case, this intellectualized and systematic irrationalism has probably never enjoyed more prestige than it does today. Sophisticated minds, many of whom applaud the social and cultural changes which the philosophy of the Enlightenment announced, are nevertheless opposed to that philosophy at its very base—not simply to its oversimplifications and its closet theories, but to the idea that it is reasonable to think of applying reason to human affairs. For two hundred years at least, during the period of its greatest power and triumphs, Western civilization has been suffering from a crisis of confidence about itself. There are many good reasons why that crisis of confidence should exist. But is the supposed fact that we have sold our souls to reason one of them?

Let us examine the philosophy of irrationalism, considering its central ideas or theses one by one. Perhaps this will help explain how apparently sane men who have lived a bit in this unreasonable world can nevertheless continue to believe in the sovereignty of human reason.

Thesis 1. Man is simply too irrational to be expected to live in accordance with reason. Most human beings, proponents of irrationalism point out, have pronounced tendencies to gullibility, hysteria, self-deception, and self-destruction. Even the most gentle and reasonable men, in fact, usually think not with their heads but with their hearts. The proposal that men live in accordance with reason is simply an unrealistic ideal. Besides, it is cold and cerebral, and inherently unattractive.

The difficulty with this thesis is not that it is false. The difficulty is that, except for its conclusion, it is so obviously true. The irrationalist repeats the truism that man is an obstinately irrational creature as though this were a new discovery. But despite the avant-garde provincialism which suggests that it has been the twentieth century's privilege to discover human unreason, the announcement that man is irrational is not news. And it does not undermine the ideal of reason. For what the irrationalist fails to do is to make an important distinction between two meanings of the word "reason."

When we speak of a man's behavior being "rational," we may mean either of two things. We may mean that he behaves in accordance with norms or purposes that we accept as sound; or we may mean that he thinks before he acts, and that his conclusions are reached by logical processes and careful and correct assessment of the relevant evidence. Needless to say, these are very different. By the first definition of "rationality"—and it is a quite normal one—a mother picking up her child when it cries, a chemist carefully washing test tubes in his laboratory, a commuter boarding the 8:15, a football player kicking a ball, are all behaving rationally.

They do not have to be conscious of the standards to which they are conforming; they do not have to be thinking about what they are doing; their behavior is certainly not the product of any nervous marshaling of arguments and fiddling with evidence; it may be purely a product of unthinking love, fussiness, habit, or unconscious illusions about the properties of pigskin. Nevertheless, just so long as their behavior meets the expected norms it is rational. It serves purposes that are desirable and intelligent purposes, and in an effective way—more effectively, very often, than if it were cerebral and self-conscious. In this sense of the term, we call men "rational" when their behavior, their overt performance, is rational, and the internal psychological processes that underlie that behavior have nothing to do with our judgment. We are interested in results, not causes.

From this point of view, there is nothing strange in the belief that man is a rational animal, and no inconsistency between this belief and recognizing how thoughtless, illogical, and dream-ridden most of us are most of the time. The great majority of men and women usually behave in perfectly rational ways, in the sense here in question. They get up in the morning, go to work, collect their pay, pay their taxes, raise their children, and see their dentist twice a year. To be sure, a very large number of people do not behave rationally even in this sense. But allowing for lapses in everybody's life, the majority of man- and woman-kind do. Nor is a rational life necessarily a spiritless or joyless affair. Dancing to hot jazz can be a perfectly rational amusement, at any rate if it is not accompanied by too much self-conscious cerebration about the importance of the instinctual life. And unless one has the standards of a prig, spontaneous fun, personal loyalty, and passionate love can all be viewed as meeting rational standards and as forming integral parts of a rational life.

Moreover, we are often perfectly justified in saying that a man is rational when, in deciding what to do, he employs processes of rational thought, but not his own. All of us do this every day. We turn to our lawyer, doctor, tax consultant, and county agent, to the cookbook, the repair manual, and Dr. Spock's book on baby care. An organized society puts countless aids to rationality at our disposal. Of course, it puts countless aids to superstition and hysteria at our disposal as well. There is an obvious need, therefore, for the individual to employ rational processes of thought when he chooses the authority to which he turns, and to use some independent judgment when he acts on the advice this authority gives him. But in many cases this merely consists in knowing to whom else to turn—friends, relatives, visiting social workers, the local clergyman—to receive advice on where to go for advice and how to use it.

This is why, incidentally, a good deal of the human irrationality that exists in the world is at bottom a socially rooted phenomenon. It reflects the absence in the individual's milieu of informed and trustworthy people to whom he can turn for honest counsel. The distribution of the opportunity to be rational, like the distribution of other opportunities, is affected by considerations of class, race, wealth, family connections, education, and political resources. Those who think that men might be more rational if a better distribution of the goods of life were achieved in society are not laboring under the misapprehension that men would thereby be converted into instant logicians. They merely think that more people might be better informed and guided by their environments than is now the case.

However, an additional question has to be raised, and a most important one. It has to do with the standards we employ when we declare behavior rational. A soldier doing his duty is behaving rationally in the sense that he is meeting accepted standards, but a pacifist may feel that these standards are mad. It is possible, and rather discouragingly easy, looking at many organized human activities that are accepted as normal, to think that the sane and sober men we see doing their jobs are simply placid, subdued inmates of a madhouse. Much irrationality in human affairs is irrationality of this kind—for example, an uncontrolled arms race, or plans to blow the human species off the planet in the interest of national defense, or defenses of such plans which assert that the human race will not be *entirely* blown off the planet but only three quarters blown off. In such cases, no one, individually, is crazy; or, at any rate, the incidence of lunacy is low. What is "mad" is the controlling standard or purpose that directs the behavior of the people concerned and which they are willing to accept.

The issue is considerably confused, however, when the nature of this sort of judgment with regard to human "irrationality" is misunderstood. When we make the judgment that men are irrational, meaning that they live by irrational standards, we are making a judgment of these standards; we have produced no evidence that the individuals concerned are mentally unhinged. That is a separate issue. Our description of the actual behavior of the people concerned is no different from the description that someone who thinks they are rational would give. So far as the facts are concerned, there is no disagreement. For we are discussing a question in moral and political philosophy, a question about the nature of a good life or a rational society. We are not discussing a question in mental hygiene or exposing the psychopathology of the ordinary individual members of the human community.

Accordingly, when an advocate of reason proposes that reason be adopted as a guide to life, he is not necessarily proposing that all of us undergo psychotherapy or become sicklied o'er with the pale cast of thought. He may be making only the *social* proposal that better, more reasonable standards than those that prevail be adopted for the governance of the community's affairs. The only psychological assumption that he makes is that, if these more reasonable standards were adopted, most people could and would abide by them. This is a large assumption; it is not, however, the utopian (and repellent) assumption that men and women will spend their time searching for facts and worrying about their reasons before ever taking any action.

Of course, a believer in reason would also hope that more men and women could and would develop the habit of rigorous thought, and would learn to assess evidence carefully before acting. For the spread of such a tendency would encourage the development in society at large of standards that reflected a more thorough and informed examination of the existing facts and possibilities of human life. But the man who hopes that human life can be made more reasonable certainly does not have to believe that men can be converted into computing machines, or that, as a daily regimen, they can govern their behavior by thinking and analyzing from dawn to dark. And still less does he have to think that this would be an agreeable state of affairs.

Nor is the failure to see that men can be rational without

becoming thinking machines the only fallacy of the irrationalist. He also commits a *non sequitur* when he proceeds from the fact of human unreason to the conclusion that the ideal of reason ought to be rejected. To say that man is irrational is a statement of fact (an ambiguous one); to say that reason ought not to be adopted as a central human ideal is a moral proposal, and it does not follow from the statement of fact. There is still a question whether we should think human unreason deplorable. If we do ever so regard it, then to that extent we accept the moral sovereignty of reason.

Thesis 2. Reason is not a motivating force in human behavior, and cannot supply the vital feelings on which moral values depend. This thesis of irrationalism is both psychological and logical. It says that reason is cold, and has no causal efficacy. It also says that reason cannot provide, by itself, logical grounds for choosing one set of values rather than another, or, indeed, for electing any values at all.

Camus's Stranger, who could find no grounds for moral commitment though he was capable of rational thought, beautifully exemplifies this thesis concerning the final, radical inadequacy of reason. And it is a perfectly sound thesis. As a philosophical proposition put forward by the irrationalist, however, it does battle with a straw man. For believers in the authority of reason can and do agree with it. Aristotle, whom no one has accused of inadequate respect for reason, observed that thought by itself moves nothing. Spinoza, one of the purest masters of philosophical rationalism in the history of philosophy, believed that only a passion could master a passion, that reason alone could conquer none of the emotions that lead men astray. David Hume, a central figure in the development of the scientific and analytic philosophies now widespread in England and America, believed that reason is, and of necessity must be, the slave of the passions. For the belief that reason should be the guide of life does not depend on the assumption that reason is a motivating force in human affairs. Nor does it depend on the idea that pure intelligence can give anyone a logically compelling reason for loving his neighbors if he is not in his heart disposed to do so.

The mention of Hume brings up, however, a genuine source of confusion. There is a long-established tradition of philosophical "rationalism," in the technical sense of the term, which has argued that it is possible to prove matters of fact by purely a priori reasoning, and which has also often argued that the fundamental values of morality can be discovered and demonstrated by acts of pure intellectual insight. Plato's philosophy is the classic example of this sort of rationalism. The irrationalist's argument is justified in so far as this tradition in thought is the target of criticism. Morals are not a form of arithmetic, and right and wrong are not matters for strict logical demonstration.

However, few contemporary spokesmen for reason would say that they are. The "rationalism" which the contemporary irrationalist condemns is a much broader point of view than technical philosophical rationalism. It is better represented by Hume, who denied that matters of fact could be known a priori or that moral truths could be established except by appealing, at least in part, to human sentiments, feelings, and desires. In this broader sense, "rationalism" is perfectly consistent with the position that reason alone can make no one, and can argue no one, into being a moral man. For reason as an intellectual process consists in the analysis and organization of ideas, and in the examination of the relationship between objective evidence and our beliefs about the facts; and neither of these is sufficient to support conclusions that have moral force. We can accept truths as truths and facts as facts, and at the same time make our own judgment of these truths or facts. The process of physical aging, for example, is what it is, and we can know it for what it is. We are still free to exercise the judgment that in most cases it is a painful and undignified affair, and not a process that any human being is compelled to approve.

A belief in reason, therefore, does not entail the belief that morals are an impersonal science. "Rationalism," in the sense in which most of its adherents understand it, consists only in the belief that reason is a proper *regulating principle* of human conduct. It is a guide, not a causal agent; it can map out the best way to reach an end, it can show what the dangers and risks are, and what the advantages are; but the dangers are dangers and the advantages advantages only because the human beings who turn to reason for guidance also have biological drives and social commitments. Reason is and must be the slave of the passions; it is from the passions that it must borrow its goals and driving force. To believe in reason is only to say that it is a better servant of the passions than wishful thinking, unexamined traditions, personal intuition, or blind faith; that men will be disappointed by it less frequently; and that they will be able to bring more harmony into their passional life with its help than with the help of other methods. For other methods generally turn out to be simply excuses for letting one passion ride roughshod over all the others.

Indeed, it is misleading to say that reason is inadequate because it is incapable of solving the ultimate puzzle as to the foundations of morality. For the puzzle is artificial. Men are biological and social creatures. The problem they face is not to work out a reason for becoming attached to life, or to develop, out of the void, some desires, aversions, hopes, and fears. They are born with certain drives, and they are born into a surrounding web of affections, obligations, and communal interests. The problem they face is to choose among these drives, interests, and obligations, to sort out and organize their commitments. It is not to invent them out of whole cloth or to justify having them to the satisfaction of an uncaring observer from Mars. This remarkably intellectualist preoccupation lies at the bottom of much of the discontent with reason. Reason, there is no doubt, cannot make the blood flow in a man; but that is not its job. Its job is to help men in whom the blood does flow to use their energies effectively.

Thesis 3. Reason is a false guide. It pretends to objectivity and impersonality, but it is in fact intensely subjective and personal. Man's conscious emotional life, and his unconscious emotional life even more, color all his thinking and make the ideal of unbiased intelligence impossible to achieve and dangerous to pursue.

The evidence which psychoanalysis, psychology, and sociology have so far been able to adduce is not adequate, I believe, to support this thesis in the sweeping form in which it is so often put forward. But it is incontestible that objectivity is a rare individual trait, and that even those who do achieve objectivity do so with great difficulty and maintain it usually only for brief periods of time. However, the nature of objective thought and judgment is not understood so long as it is conceived in purely individual and psychological terms. This is the central error in the attack on reason as a "false guide."

Objectivity in thought and judgment, generally speaking, is a social achievement, the product of long co-operative processes of controlled questioning, communication, and mutual criticism. The sciences in particular represent such inherited, self-correcting social disciplines; but social aids to objectivity can also be found in the traditions of regulated argument that characterize other fields of learning. It is in subordinating one's personal preferences and beliefs to the discipline of argument and of public examination by a community of trained and competent critics that one is helped to escape the influence of one's own personal bias. To deny that anyone ever successfully does so is to deny that men by cooperative effort have ever managed to achieve any reliable, impersonal—which is to say, interpersonal—knowledge of anything in their world. It is to adopt a grotesque view of the human condition for the sake of a melodramatic paradox.

Indeed, the view that reason by its very nature is a false guide is a basic self-contradiction. It is not possible to assign meaning to the idea of being "biased" unless meaning can be given to the idea of being "unbiased." The statement that there is no such thing as objectivity is itself a pretender to the throne of objectivity. For if it is merely an expression of personal bias, it deserves no further consideration as a contribution to the public, cooperative analysis of a difficult issue. On the other hand, if it is intended to be a contribution to such an analysis, it presupposes that there really is some sense, after all, in speaking of objectivity as though it were something at which human beings might aim.

Thesis 4. Reason is an enemy of insight and originality, a method of subduing the individual to the dictatorship of the collective. "Democratic resentment," says Professor Brown, "denies that there can be anything that can't be seen by everybody; in the democratic academy truth is subject to public verification; truth is what any fool can see. This is what is meant by the so-called scientific method: so-called science is the attempt to democratize knowledge—the attempt to substitute method for insight, mediocrity for genius, by getting a standard operating procedure. The great equalizers dispensed by the scientific method are the tools, those analytical tools. The miracle of genius is replaced by the standardized mechanism. But fools with tools are still fools, and don't let your Phi Beta Kappa keys fool you."

But as anyone who has tried to master calculus or organic chemistry without the necessary aptitude can testify, truth in the sciences just does not happen to be what any fool can see. Of course, you must indeed reach results with which others will agree. You must put your evidence and reasoning before these others and allow them to see if they come to the same conclusions. But the critical audience to which you address your work is a trained audience, made up of people who have demonstrated the by no means universal capacity to use the special language and instruments of the sciences in accordance with the rules. This does not substitute method for insight, or mediocrity for genius. Leibniz, Newton, and Einstein were not beaten down to the level of the herd because their insights passed rational muster.

The key issue here, in fact, goes beyond purely intellectual matters. It has to do with the etiquette of human intercourse and communication. When a man says that he *knows* something, he is not merely saying that he happens to have an opinion, or that he has had an impressive experience, or that he holds strong feelings. He is saying that others ought to think as he does; he is making a claim on the minds of his fellows. But why should his fellows grant this claim if he will not put his cards on the table? What goes for poker goes for fair dealing in matters of the mind as well.

Professor Brown speaks of "mysteries" in which genuine truth reposes, and says that these mysteries are "unpublishable," first, because "they cannot be put into words," and, second, because "only some can see them, not all." Very well; he may have his mysteries; reason, surely, cannot argue him out of them. But if he asks others to accept these mysteries, if he calls for an intellectual revolution which will restore mysteries to the center of the intellectual life, he is offering nothing more than his own say-so to support these enormous demands. The condemnation of reason because it seeks to bring men into agreement by appealing to public, external evidence is incompatible not only with the conditions of orderly inquiry. It is incompatible with elementary demands of courtesy.

Much that is said in criticism of the analytic methods of reason, and of the limitations of the rules of logic in a world whose realities always outrun the categories of the human mind, fails to take account of this point. Reason is, among other things, a social etiquette, a manner of conducting human communication so that men can work cooperatively toward common ends. If we wish others to understand us, we have to use our terms with a consistent meaning. If we wish to make definite intellectual progress, rejecting beliefs on which we do not think it safe to act together and determining just where we are willing to place our bets, we have to formulate our ideas with sufficient sharpness and precision so that it is possible to say of them that they are either true or false, and that they must be one or the other. The basic rules of logic—the principles of "identity," "contradiction," and "excluded middle"—are not descriptions either of nature or of the psychological processes of the human mind. They are rules for the regulation of human discourse, and there is no law of nature that says we must obey them. The penalty if we don't is simply that we will not communicate to our fellows and will not make cooperative progress in finding beliefs on which we can, on impersonal grounds, agree. And the same is true for the tendency of rational inquiry to analyze and dissect what it studies. Only by isolating selected features of what we are studying, only by concentrating attention, can we fix what we are saying precisely enough to know just what we are talking about.

This is not to deny the right of any individual to live by incommunicable mysteries. It is certainly not to say that his deepest feelings have no value, or that his intuitions are any less rich or compelling to him than they are. It is merely to say that his feelings and intuitions, and his mysteries, can make no claim on the assent of others. It is to say that he cannot say that he *knows.* He does not, it should always be remembered, have to say this; he can enjoy his soliloquies in his solitude. But if he does ask that others credit them as clues to the truth, he enters a domain in which rules of social communication take over. He has asked others to agree with him because there are strong impersonal reasons for doing so. Under these circumstances, strong personal convictions, no matter what elevated or esoteric term is used to designate them, are irrelevant. Fools with tools may still be fools, but to be without tools, and mindless of all rules, does not prove you are wise.

Thesis 5. The belief in reason is a form of hubris. It encour- ages a belief in human infallibility and in the infinitude of man's powers. William Barrett has given a typical statement of this thesis. "The finitude of man, as established by Heidegger," he writes, "is perhaps the death blow to the ideology of the Enlightenment, for to recognize this finitude is to acknowledge that man will always exist in untruth as well as truth. . . . The realization that all human truth must not only shine against an enveloping darkness, but that such truth is even shot through with its own darkness may be depressing, and not only to utopians. But it has the virtue of restoring to man his sense of the primal mystery surrounding all things, a sense of mystery from which the glittering world of his technology estranges him, but without which he is not truly human."[3]

A primal mystery among the primal mysteries, however, is just what those who make this statement—and it is made very frequently—are actually saying. For they appear to be launching an assault on a fortress which modern adherents of reason have long since finished attacking and destroying. The finitude of man, "as established by Heidegger," Mr. Barrett says, apparently in all solemnity. But it would not occur to the average contemporary believer in reason to imagine that the finitude of man needed to be established, let alone by the arguments of Heidegger. It is the sort of fact, one would imagine, that every peasant knows.

The principle that all human beliefs about the nature of the world are subject to future correction is a cornerstone of modern scientific procedure and of modern rationalism in the broad sense of the term. Far from announcing that man is infallible, the modern, empirically oriented belief in reason denies that there are *any* methods—whether we call them "revelation," "in-

[3] William Barrett, *Irrational Man* (New York: Doubleday and Co., 1958), p. 244.

tuition," or "knowing in one's bones"—that give men infallible insights into the nature of things. The preference for "reason" is a preference for a method that begins with an acknowledgment of the limitations of human intelligence, and builds into itself safeguards against erecting into unassailable absolutes the answers that anyone's intelligence accepts at a given moment. And by the same token, a guiding principle of rational inquiry is that no a priori limits can be set to what man is capable of discovering. This does not imply that man can be omniscient or that any of the answers he finds to the problems he sets himself will be free from the possibility of error. It means only that we can never say of any particular problem, if it is intelligibly formulated, that it cannot be solved. The limits of human knowledge are indefinite precisely because we *are* fallible, and can never know enough to proclaim, with regard to any particular problem, that our ignorance is invincible.

But reason itself, it is often argued, has now demonstrated in a peculiarly powerful way that, with regard to certain questions, it is faced with insoluble paradoxes. Reason has therefore had to admit, as reason has never had to admit before, so it is said, that it must bow down before the ultimate mystery of things. Those who make this argument usually have in mind such technical aspects of modern physics and mathematics as Heisenberg's Principle of Indeterminacy and Gödel's analysis of the possibility of establishing the consistency of mathematical systems. It would take considerable space to show in adequate detail how the irrationalist misconceives the nature and purport of such achievements of modern rational inquiry. A brief discussion of the issues posed by these scientific achievements, however, may help place them in proper perspective.

Heisenberg's Principle of Indeterminacy shows that, in dealing with certain kinds of subatomic phenomena, it is not possible to fix precisely both the velocity and the position of individual particles. Contrary to prevailing interpretations, however, this does not show that explanation and prediction are impossible, or that, in the subatomic world, there is a "free," "indeterminist," "trans-rational" element at play. It merely upsets one classic conception of "determinism," one classic way of thinking about explanation and prediction—the way of thinking supplied by nineteenth-century mechanics—and offers a new pattern of explanation and prediction, applicable to certain special areas of physics.

Similarly, Gödel's proof, despite popular misstatements of it, does not demonstrate that the consistency of mathematical systems—for example, the language of arithmetic—cannot be proved. It makes the much more refined point that such a proof cannot be represented *within* the language of arithmetic. Far from indicating that there are immovable limits to human reason, Gödel's proof indicates the contrary principle, that the resources of the human mind cannot be caught in any one formal mathematical or logical calculus, and that there is no telling what new principles of invention and discovery are still to see the light of day. By and large, Heisenberg's principle carries the same human moral. Neither testifies either to the ultimate incapacity of the mind or to its potential omniscience; they testify to its continuing potential for invention, discovery, and self-transcendence. They do not justify *hubris,* because they make every achievement of the human intellect seem small in the light of what may be achieved in the future. But neither do they justify melancholia about the human intellect—which is *hubris* turned petulant—for they show what that intellect can achieve.

"The primal mystery surrounding all things" is a portentous

phrase. If it refers to anything at all beyond the fact that our knowledge is always incomplete, it presumably means only that there is no ultimate explanation of why things are as they are and not otherwise. The nature and contents of the world that exists cannot be shown to be logically necessary; that our world is as it is, is simply a contingent fact, something for which we can give no all-inclusive, final explanation. We can explain a given event by placing it in a system of laws. When asked why these laws are as they are, we can answer by connecting them with a more embracing system of laws. And we can go on and on, but at some point we are going to have to stop and say that we know no more, that we have gone as far as, at the moment, we can go. This is a position which is in thorough accord with that of modern empirical rationalism. The difference is only that the irrationalist describes this state of affairs as a "primal mystery." But why should he do so? All that has been shown is that no matter what explanation we give of events, no matter how we answer the question Why? it is always possible to ask for a further explanation. If the irrationalist finds this fact about human knowledge a primal mystery, this reveals that he continues to think that the ideal of absolute, infallible, and final knowledge makes sense. He is, in other words, a philosophical rationalist in the pure Platonic sense of the term—a philosophical rationalist *manqué*. The believers in human reason whom the irrationalist attacks for their *hubris* do not make the demands on human intelligence that he does—which is why they do not announce that their hearts are broken by the discovery of "human finitude."

Thesis 6. Reason is analytic, dissective, and discursive. It cuts up the living reality, and puts into words what eludes all words.

It therefore offers an incurably false portrait of things. Silence, as Heidegger observes, is the authentic mode of speech. Or, in Kierkegaard's phrase, "The surest way of being mute is not to hold your tongue, but to talk."

This is probably the most fundamental thesis of intellectual irrationalism. And it is a theatrical way of stating certain homely truths. Talking about a thing, it cannot be denied, is not the same thing as being that thing. Nor is the analysis or description of a feeling or an experience identical with having that feeling or experience. Knowing is not eating, as Santayana remarks, and we cannot be expected to devour what we mean. For knowing, reasoning, and talking inevitably involve us in abstractions, and abstractions select and organize only certain features of a subject matter.

To be sure, language has other functions besides abstract intellectual explanation. Words can be used as cues to what lies beyond them, as ways of evoking emotions and images, as parts of a liturgy of joy or sorrow, as instruments of communion and comradeship. "The fact that certain great novelists have chosen to write in terms of images rather than of arguments," Camus wrote, "reveals a great deal about a certain kind of thinking common to them all, a conviction of the futility of all explanatory principles, and of the instructive message of sensory impressions." If this means that sensory impressions can produce feelings and sensitivities that abstractions will not produce, the statement is true. But it does not make a case against reason or explanatory principles. For this would be to reject them on the irrelevant ground that they do not perform other functions than those to which they are adapted. It is like asking that a menu be equivalent to a meal.

The fallacy in the irrationalist condemnation of abstractions

lies in the failure to see that abstractions would serve no purpose at all if they were not selective, and if they were not separate from what they are about—if they were not, in a word,
abstractions. Their separateness from their subject matter and
their selective isolation of certain of its features are precisely the
reasons why they bring order to what would otherwise be
inchoate, brute experience. Rational knowledge, communicated
in words, is of course not a surrogate for love, or for a feeling of
communion with someone else, or for ecstasy, or for immersion
in the flux of experience. But neither are these surrogates for
knowledge. No one can take quite literally the pompous remark
that silence is the authentic mode of speech. If this is true, then
giraffes are studies in eloquence and oysters give lessons in wisdom. Intellectual communication is not the only form of communication, and other forms are precious and indispensable.
But so is intellectual communication. To attack words and
abstractions wholesale is to attack civilization, and one can only
assume that those who make such attacks are consciously exaggerating for the sake of effect.

No doubt there is provocation for the assault on abstractions
in which so many philosophers, theologians, and humanists are
presently engaged. In our highly organized and rationalized
society, the tendency exists to make judgments without apparent realization of the human emotions, and the dense, textured
human situations, that are hidden by abstract formulas. There
is a kind of desiccated simulacrum—almost a parody—of rational
thought in which some apostles of "scientific method" in human affairs unquestionably indulge. The application of the
theory of games to questions of thermonuclear war by writers
like Herman Kahn is an example. But the reason that the
theory of games is a misleading tool to apply to thermonuclear

war is that the assumptions that have to be made in order to use the theory are unrealistic. In this sense, its fault is not that it is abstract but, as common parlance puts it, "too abstract." And this is a matter to be discovered, established, and communicated by intellectual means. Similarly, if technological and bureaucratic arrangements are "viciously abstract," if they ignore legitimate values and crush out the singularities of men, this too is a matter that can only be discovered or changed by orderly processes of thought. Silence will simply not do, not even the wordy, book-length silence of irrationalist philosophers.

Thesis 7. Reason generalizes, and is therefore inapplicable to the study and guidance of human affairs, for men are characterized by their originality and uniqueness. According to this point of view, it is foolish to imagine, as the devotee of reason does, that general laws can be discovered which explain human behavior. Such laws would apply only to puppets. Man, who is creative and who has free will, eludes all efforts to categorize him.

There is little doubt that some extraordinarily simplistic efforts to explain human behavior have been made by people eager to find a pattern in human affairs. But it is the grossest misconception of the nature of generalizations about human affairs to imagine that they foreclose the possibilities for originality or individual idiosyncrasy. If people are the same in certain respects, then they are the same in those respects, and that just happens to be that. All of us depend on oxygen to live, on the circulation of the blood, on taking in food. And there are also certain common patterns in our behavior that are social in character rather than biological. All of us, to take a commonplace example, *learn* a language. None of us learns to speak

unless someone speaks to him. But if people resemble one another in these or other respects, this does not mean that they
cannot differ as well. Each of us, after all, speaks a common
language with his own special accent. No generalization rules
out idiosyncrasy, and human idiosyncrasy does not make all
generalization invalid.

*Thesis 8. There are other things in life besides reason. A man
who merely relies on abstract thought is likely to be cold to
significant human values.* There is a great difference, after all, it
is commonly pointed out, between what the physical scientist
does in his laboratory and what the historian does when he tries
to explain why a statesman acted as he did or why a nation
suddenly broke apart in civil war. A child can report a pointer
reading; only a man who has lived and reflected and had a
variety of human emotions can give a judicious explanation of
human history.

There is, indeed, a difference, even though it is doubtful that
a child could set up the experiment of which the pointer reading is a part or interpret the significance of what he reports. Still,
a relevant and intelligent discussion of human affairs unquestionably requires special experience, imagination, and feeling,
and although the creative practice of a natural science requires
such qualities too, it does not require experience in human
affairs or refinement of human feeling (though it does not pre-
clude them). Once more, however, the irrationalist makes a
point that has nothing to do with the applicability of rational
methods to the study of human affairs. For it is *irrational* to
ignore any aspects of human experience which are relevant to
understanding human behavior. If refinement of sensibility and
a developed imagination lead to the detection of the lights and

shadows of human affairs, then they are indispensable instruments of progress in the understanding of events. But they are instruments of reason, not alternatives to it. They make it more probable that relevant matters will be examined. They do not take the place of orderly thought or the dispassionate appraisal of evidence.

Something much more than meets the eye generally lies behind the irrationalist appeal to "other values" besides reason. In invoking "other values"—human sympathy, aesthetic appreciation, mystic insight, feelings of religious reverence—the irrationalist does not mean only to say that these *are* values. Commonly, he means also to say that they are paths to the discovery of significant truths, that the use of reason is incompatible with the discovery of these truths, and that these truths carry their own certificates of validity. And this position rests on a confusion between the *genesis* of ideas and the *test* of their truth.

Men may come to true ideas in any number of ways, from daydreaming to sudden flashes of inspiration. Those who have come to original conceptions by a harsh, step-by-step process of logical analysis and empirical investigation are in fact relatively few. Intuitive leaps are much more common in the history of creative thought. But there are many intuitive leaps that are leaps into falsehood, and rather a large number of mystic intuitions that have yielded only dispiriting banalities. Independent and impersonal standards are required to evaluate the results of thought, no matter what kind of thought is involved. The irrationalist demand that "other values" be respected is merely the demand that some ideas be free from the test of such independent standards.

Indeed, a peculiar kind of value judgment appears to be involved in irrationalism. The insistence that "other values" besides reason be respected as sources of truth reflects a curious unwillingness to grant value to any aspects of human life unless they can be shown to have a cognitive function. The paradigmatic case of this effort to reduce all important values to intellectual values is the philosophy of Plato, in which poetry and love are assigned significance as vehicles to the truth, even though they are of lesser significance than philosophy. But few contemporary believers in reason would make such demands on these departments of human life, which surely have their own reasons for being even if they do not contribute to the progress of human knowledge. In the end, it is the irrationalist who downgrades affection, spontaneity, reverence, and love, for he will not accept them in their own terms for the valuable things they are. It is the irrationalist, not the rationalist, who suffers from excessive intellectualism.

Since the time of the French Revolution, it has been usual to make reason a principal culprit when explanations have been offered of the troubles of the modern world. The French Revolution itself, according to a continuing line of historical interpretation, was the work and the catastrophe of reason. The horrors that accompanied it were not due to normal human vanity or to abnormal social resentments. They were not the products of intelligible fears of foreign invasion and of internal subversion. They were not even due to the abuse of reason—to the inexperience and arrogance of the revolutionaries, or to their oversimplified, coffeehouse political ideas. They were due to the belief in reason itself, to the insane passion to regulate human affairs by the rule of reason. And similar interpretations have been offered of every subsequent revolution that has taken place in the revolutionary West, and in the now revolutionary Westernized East.

The theory that the belief in reason is a form of madness is at the base, indeed, of a general theory of modern history. In the works of Nietzsche, Toynbee, Ortega y Gasset, and many others, it has been developed into the point of departure for a comprehensive interpretation of the meaning of Western life and experience since the breakdown of the feudal era. And the belief that we have given our souls away to mechanistic and lifeless reason has been used by countless students of modern society to explain why our industry is so impersonal, our cities so inhuman and ugly, our scholarship so pedantic, our culture so homogenized.

Probably no other idea has more to do with the generalized anxiety that Western culture is fundamentally on the wrong footing. Certainly this conception of reason is a major source of the endemic sense of alienation that characterizes so many Western intellectuals, who find themselves not merely radical critics of modern society and culture but helpless and disarmed critics. For they cannot accept the alternatives, for thought and action and discriminate choice, that are available to us. Yet the idea of reason which leaves them thus disarmed and helpless is not an idea that withstands analysis.

III

———⚜———

The Family in Context

THE FAMILY, BY COMMON CONSENT, IS A CENTRAL INSTITUTION OF our society. It is regarded as the principal setting in which individual personality is formed, and is probably the most cherished —or, at any rate, the most widely praised—institution of our civilization. Yet, paradoxically enough, there is no great classic in twentieth-century social theory, comparable to Max Weber's study of bureaucracy or to Gunnar Myrdal's study of American race relations, that is devoted to the family. It has been studied at length and in the greatest detail. That it is undergoing immense transformations is recognized. But no general estimate of its condition, or its strengths, weaknesses, and prospects, exists.

I can claim no special knowledge of the family, and what I propose to set forth is certainly much less than a theory of the family. What I wish to do is to discuss two questions about it. First, what are the fundamental changes in our institutions and attitudes that have affected the family and produced the situation in which we now find it? Second, what is the value of the family, the purpose, that is to say, which we should have in mind when we say that the family is worth preserving and strengthening, and when we set about trying to do so?

Let me begin by stating the thesis which I wish to demonstrate and explore. It is this: the family in Western society was once the principal agency for the performance of what are now called welfare functions; it is now the principal target of these functions. It has been converted from the doctor to the patient. What is involved in this change? What has caused it? What new attitudes and what new social conceptions are required to deal effectively with this problem?

The answers to these questions lie in a complex of fundamental and radical changes which have taken place in Western society over the past three or four hundred years. Principal among these are the shift from an agricultural subsistence economy to a commercial economy; industrialization; the steady movement of displaced rural people to the cities; what I shall call the "Americanization" of culture; the rise of liberal ideas concerning the proper relation of the individual to the social groups in which he is born or to which he becomes attached; and last, the democratization of the once aristocratic ideal of romantic love. A glance at each of these may help us to see the problem of the family in its context.

The shift from an agricultural subsistence economy to a commercial economy is the first step in the major secular trend that has marked the development of the modern family. That trend is the steady expulsion of the family from the economy and, in a certain sense, from society. In traditional agricultural societies, the family is an economic unit, the principal social instrument of production. Children, especially male children, are economically profitable rather than burdensome. And large, extended families, consisting of grandparents, uncles, aunts, cousins, and in-laws as well as children, are forms of social insurance, the

basic protection against the blows of sickness, old age, and out-
rageous fortune. Accordingly, the individual's experience
within his family is at the same time his principal experience of
society at large. In giving him his name, the family also gives
him his place—usually his lifetime place—in society. It is as a
member of a family that the individual not simply learns his
social roles but acquires them. And it is within his family that
he does the work of the world.

The commercialization of the economy, in contrast, brings
strangers together. It begins to separate the home from the
economy and, indeed, to give the home its modern meaning as a
refuge away from practical problems rather than a device for
dealing with these problems. Commercialization, furthermore,
brings in its train standard instruments of exchange like money,
impersonal instruments of social control like the police and
government officials, uniform and explicit rules and regulations
like delivery schedules, piecework rates, and systems of cost ac-
counting. These may not quite destroy the traditional powers of
the elders of the clan nor the traditional habit of treating one's
kinsmen differently from the stranger. But they break into such
powers and habits and put them under the pressure to justify
themselves. The traditional family is held together by a system
of authority based largely on a man's "natural"—which is to say,
culturally inherited—status as the elder or the father. The
commercialization of a society begins to introduce the notion
that status and authority are acquired by performance rather
than simply ascribed. Traditional notions of authority, based on
the family, lose their monopolistic position. Internal authority
within the family is affected.

The industrialization of society immensely quickened this
process. As a student of the industrialization of modern China

has remarked, "Modern industry and the 'traditional' family are mutually subversive."[1] Industrialization took work farther away from the home. Just as much to the point, it took women and children out of the home, and affected the position of the male as the principal director of the economic and educational life of the family. Industrialization, furthermore, tends to change the traditional extended family from a necessity to a source of irritation. Viewed from the standpoint of industrialization, the traditional extended family makes mobility more difficult. It enlarges the circle of dependents for whom the individual is responsible. It limits his associations and circumscribes the activities in which he ought to participate if he wishes to improve his condition. Not least, the traditional extended family preserves the idea that the old have a function to serve in the family; industrialism, in contrast, declares the old obsolete.

Industrialization, furthermore, is in part the invention of techniques for invention, and perhaps the deepest of its effects lies in the steadily accelerating tempo of social change which it creates. It produces a world in which the generations feel more separate, more distant, from one another, and creates reasonable doubts in both parents and children that the old can give the young useful lessons in how to make their way in the world. Even a hundred years ago, the grandmother who knew her place was a matriarch. Now, if she is lucky and moves as though she were treading on eggshells, she may just barely qualify as a friend. No doubt there have always been quarrels between children and parents. But industrialization, for better or worse, makes this a structural feature of human history.

[1] Marion J. Levy, Jr., *The Family Revolution in Modern China* (Cambridge: Harvard University Press, 1949).

Nor is this all. Industrialization is linked with urbanization, which reinforces the tendencies toward the miniaturization of the family and the loosening of the bonds within it. The living space in cities is crowded and expensive, and particularly so for those families undergoing the greatest stresses of transition. Quite simply, the large family, stretching over more than two generations, does not fit into city apartments, or, if it is made to fit, the fit is painful and can be the source of new and steady frictions. Moreover, the dwellers in cities are mobile, physically and psychologically. They go where the jobs are, and their minds move in larger orbits. Their ties to a particular neighborhood or to their own parental family are weaker as a consequence. Cities are towns with floating populations; and they are also the scenes of a recurrent drama—the conflict between the first generation of new arrivals and the second generation, which has rejected the old traditions and is tempted, frightened, resentful, or greedy when it contemplates the life that lies beyond the ghetto.

Nor are commerce, technology, and industry the only factors in producing social mobility and the mobile personality. Social mobility, movement up and down the social ladder, is indeed immensely accelerated by industrialism. But something else, something nonmaterial, has also changed men's perspectives and expectations, particularly in the United States. One of the classic functions of the traditional family is simply to give the individual a name, and with that name a status which marks him for life. But the recurrent theme of the modern novel, from the time of Cervantes, is the story of the man who gives himself a name, who aspires to a position to which he has no inherited right. The familial outlook, the outlook that puts each person in his proper place by looking at his origins, is in conflict with the industrial and democratic outlook, which treats a man's status as something to be acquired and earned. And nowhere has this attitude gone further than in the United States.

Defined in strict and narrow terms, in terms, for example, of the movement of children of manual workers to white-collar jobs, social mobility in the United States is not significantly higher than social mobility in other highly industrialized countries.[2] But in America social mobility is expected and perceived; Americans believe that the process takes place, and they believe in the process. They believe, that is to say, that social mobility, the movement of free men up and down the social ladder in accordance with their abilities, is the major mechanism for achieving social justice. The achievement of social justice by conflict between social classes composed of people locked into position inside their class has not usually occurred to Americans as a normal phenomenon, and has practically never appealed to them as a desirable one. This is part of a charcteristic and persisting American style, one that can be detected very early in our history and one which has not greatly altered despite all that has happened to the structure of American society.

This, if you will, is the Americanization of culture, the acid that has corroded traditional social relationships since the colonization of North America and the emergence of the American Republic. Perhaps more than anything else, it is what America represented to the imaginations of restless millions in the nineteenth century. "The young American," said Max Weber, "has no respect for anything or anybody, for tradition or for public

2 See Reinhard Bendix and S. M. Lipset, *Social Mobility in Industrial Society* (Berkeley: University of California Press, 1959).

office—unless it is the personal achievement of individual men. This is what the American calls 'democracy.' "[3] And Baedeker's guide warily warned the European traveler coming to this country at the turn of the century that he "should, from the outset, reconcile himself to the absence of deference, of servility, on the part of those he considers his social inferiors."[4]

The effects of this attitude on the traditional patterns of authority within the family were noted long before John Dewey came on the scene, or popular versions of the doctrines of a Viennese doctor made "permissiveness" the rationale for a new form of tyranny in the home. "The theory of the equality of man is rampant in the nursery," a British visitor to the United States remarked in 1898.[5] And Arthur Calhoun has documented the changes that took place in the American family long before the Civil War.[6] The Americanization of culture meant a change in normal attitudes within the family: it meant a shift from a past-oriented family to a future-oriented one, from a parent-oriented family to a child-oriented, and some think a childishly oriented, family.

In older societies a man took pride in his son if he could imagine his son coming to share some of his own adult burdens, carrying his load in the family, carrying on the family in its work. In modern societies, and overwhelmingly in modern American society, fathers look to their sons to lift the family, to renovate it, to make it something it has not been before. And that orientation, it should be mentioned in passing, is arising

3 "Science as a Vocation," in H. H. Gerth and C. Wright Mills, ed. *From Max Weber* (London: Kegan Paul, French, Trubner and Co., 1947).
4 Quoted by S. M. Lipset, "A Changing American Character?" Institute of Industrial Relations, Reprint No. 180, University of California, 1962.
5 J. F. Muirhead, *America, the Land of Contrasts*. Quoted by Lipset, *op. cit.*
6 Arthur W. Calhoun, *A Social History of the American Family* (Cleveland: Arthur H. Clark Co., 1918).

rapidly in other societies today. The much-discussed "revolution of rising expectations" is in the first instance a demand on the part of countless men and women that their children have a chance for an education which they themselves did not have. It represents a revolution in what men and women want for their children, in the way in which they perceive their relations to their children and the rightful prospects of their children—a revolution, in a word, in the way in which they think about the nature and function of the family itself.

Closely connected with this Americanization of culture is the influence of the liberal revolution in ideas that began in the seventeenth century, came to full intellectual expression in the eighteenth, and changed the social map of Europe and America in the nineteenth. In its moral aspect, this revolution spoke for a simple idea: the idea that all authority exercised by human beings over other human beings is always only provisional authority—fallible, limited, subject to reversal when it fails to serve the functions for which it exists. It was and is a radical idea, one that had been glimpsed and expounded previously but never happily adopted as a guide for the proper organization of large societies and the government of men in all classes. And in its social aspects, this liberal idea meant a profound change in the relation of the individual to the groups to which he belongs.

It meant that the ideal relationship was normally construed as one that was revocable and alterable, a relationship that the individual could choose, and could continue to choose, for himself. The elimination of fixed feudal bonds, the protection of freedom of association and of the right to pick up and move, the easing of divorce laws, the attack on restrictive practices in inheritance, the protection of the rights of children, are all examples of this process. The liberal revolution could not quite make the family an entirely voluntary association. No one can choose his parents, or his sisters, cousins, and aunts, no matter what the law may do to enhance his freedom of choice as a citizen. But the liberal revolution went a long way in changing the family from a wholly hereditary grouping into one with many more elements of voluntary association in it. It reinforced, and was reinforced by, the material changes that were also transforming the family and converting it from a major instrument for the protection of individuals and the assignment of social status and function to only one such instrument among many.

And to this a change in moral attitudes was added. The word "love" is a dangerous word to define, and as those who remember their Plato will recall, philosophers particularly have done remarkable things with it and to it. But for our prosaic purposes, we may define it, perhaps, as an intense attraction between two people (hopefully, erotic in its character) which leads them, for a period of unspecified duration, to wish to organize their lives and their emotions around it. Some recent social theorists, bravely setting themselves against the notion that everything is learned at the bosom of "culture" and that men and women have no ideas of their own where their instincts are concerned, have gone so far as to argue that this inconvenient feeling breaks out in all societies and causes trouble in most.[7] And this may be: certainly I am not querulous enough to wish to argue against this mournful, though somehow encouraging, speculation. Nevertheless, no student of human societies has as yet denied that we in Western civiliza-

[7] See William J. Goode, "The Sociology of the Family," in Merton, Broom, and Cottrell, *Sociology Today* (New York: Basic Books, 1959).

tion have developed a special cult around the idea of love, and that this cult—the cult of romantic love—is one of the places where instinct has combined with imagination to make trouble for parents, priests, bankers, Socialists, and everyone else who favors a sensible, businesslike approach to human affairs.

The cult of romantic love, to cut a long story very short, holds that nothing is more important than love, that love justifies all. It is the secularized and materialized version of Dante's religious attitude toward Beatrice, whom he transfigured into a representative of the supernatural, a guide who could show him the way through Paradise. This is a heavy burden for one human being to place on another, and in the early stages of romantic love it was in fact a relationship that was maintained by keeping the lovers at a distance, a relationship, in other words, that was more a matter of mind than of matter. What we now know as romantic love began, indeed, as courtly love, which in its standard form was the unconsummated love of a bachelor knight for an aristocratic married lady. In the second stage of its historical career, romantic love, however, was adulterous love, based on the notion that love and marriage, to diverge from contemporary wisdom, go together like a wild horse and carriage.

This was too much, as one can imagine, for the bourgeois soul. When the middle classes took over the world, they took over romantic love and domesticated it. It was conceived as an emotion properly felt only between two otherwise uncommitted individuals, and the proper prelude to marriage. In short, romantic love, which began as an aristocratic affair providing an outlet from marriage, has ended as a plebeian affair which, in theory, is the only good reason for marriage. The cult of romantic love caps and sanctifies the great transformation in the meaning of marriage in Western society. From a practical and useful alliance of two families it has been converted into an alliance between two individuals with respect to which, so a major ethical ideal of our culture tells us, it is somehow improper and unfeeling to ask questions about practicality and use.

These, then, are some of the long-range developments that have altered the meaning and function of the family in our civilization. And during the past generation a variety of other changes have still further complicated the problem. Domestic servants have largely disappeared from middle-class homes. A larger number of women are working. The lowering of the retirement age and the technological displacement of older workers has cut still further into the authority within the family once enjoyed by the elders of the tribe. Wars have added to mobility, to quick marriages, to long separations, to a general atmosphere of unease and insecurity. The mass media of communication have moved into the home itself, changing the character of the time families spend together. And as a result of labor laws that keep youth out of the labor market, and of technical innovations which require longer and longer periods of schooling, the episode in life we know as youth, the interval between arrival at biological maturity and arrival at a recognized status as an independent adult, has been greatly extended —so much so that problems we could once sweep under the carpet, problems affecting our touchiest moral beliefs, can no longer be ignored. A larger number of those who can afford to do so marry young, taking a more frankly experimental view of marriage. Those who cannot afford the proprieties, or who take marriage too seriously to marry lightly, make other arrangements, and except for occasional outbursts at meetings devoted to the problems of youth most of us look the other way.[8]

But perhaps the greatest assault on our peace of mind comes from the simple fact that the dominant ideal of the family—the middle-class ideal of the secure family of firmly married parents with two or three children, living in a community of more or less permanent residence—this ideal, though we cling to it, is more conspicuously unrelated to the facts than ever before. Not only does it mislead us about the facts, but it imposes a single standard, and often an unrealistic and confusing standard, on the great variety of conditions and relationships that character-ize families today. On the one side, we have no developed in-tellectual theories about the family; on the other side, we are in the grip of massive stereotypes. We speak of *"the* family" as though we knew just what we meant and as though there were only one kind of entity to which it referred.

In fact, "the family" is a term that covers a wide range of disparate phenomena. There is the traditional extended family and the small, nuclear family. There is the nuclear family in which the parents are divorced; the family in which the parents are officially separated; the family in which they are neither separated nor not separated, but only intermittently together; the family in which one parent is dead; the foster family; the family in which the children have never known their father; the family in which, as a result of divorce and remarriage, there are two fathers or two mothers. And within all these different vari-eties—and there are others as well—there are further differences in ethnic origin and social class which affect the roles of parents and children and the tone and content of family life. Indeed,

8 For a study of changing sexual mores, see Ira L. Reiss, *Premarital Sexual Standards in America* (Glencoe, Ill.: The Free Press, 1960).

one of the greatest problems affecting the future welfare of what we choose to call "the family" is the persistence of the notion that there is one proper model for the family, and that all efforts to repair the condition of the family should be guided by this single conception of what it is to be a proper family.

In sum, the trials and tribulations of modern families arise, for the most part, because modern social arrangements, on the one side, have stripped the family of many of its traditional functions and patterns of authority while, on the other side, modern moral attitudes have greatly raised the emotional demands we make upon the family. The situation is one which invites a fundamental question. What is the value of the family? In trying to preserve family institutions, are we simply trying to preserve old superstitions? It is worth asking this radically skeptical question. It may help us to be clearer about the reasons behind any programs we may wish to institute to strengthen the family.

Most of the answers that are given to this question, it seems to me, are not quite to the point. It is true that families do many important things. They provide emotional support for their members, the opportunity for sexual gratification, a setting for the birth, nurturing, and rearing of children; in all probability, they are the most important agency in our society for the molding of personality and the social control of individual behavior, particularly among the young. But families are not alone in serving these functions, and many families do not serve such functions or serve them badly. Assuming that we had no deep-seated religious and moral attitudes toward the family, can we be sure that some other sort of institution might not do better?

To ask this question is to bring out, I think, the root element in the concept of "family." It is the simple idea of kinship. Families are groups of people connected by ties of blood. Even the existence of the institution of adoption, which simulates kinship, emphasizes this point. What the family does distinctively is to give the individual a name, a plain and ineffaceable tie to generations past and future, a unique locale in society. A man's family is like the color of his eyes, or, if you prefer, like the birthmark on his face. He can like it or hate it, exploit it or disguise it or perform a kind of surgery to get rid of it; but it is one of the arbitrary facts of his life. He has to live with it or take positive and painful steps to live without it. The family, the kin group, gives support to some people; it is a nuisance to others and a disaster to some. But whatever its effects on the individual, it is not a relationship which can just be assumed or rejected. A man can leave his job, and that is his own business; he can make friendships and break them, and that too is his business. But while he can leave his family or ignore his parents or children, that is not just his business. In the family he finds a kind of relationship to others that is not so easily altered as his other relationships, a set of obligations that are not provisional but categorical. The kin group gives the individual other people to whom he belongs and who belong to him, whether he likes it or not.

In short, the family introduces into our increasingly rationalized society an element of sheer inescapable contingency and individuality. A steadily larger part of our social arrangements assign interchangeable individuals to general social tasks. The worth of our arrangements is measured in terms of precisely defined utilities. The positions we occupy or the jobs we perform rest on our specific skills and services, real or alleged. The groups to which we belong are supposed to contribute to our advantage and we to theirs. The family, in contrast, envelops the individual in a network of relationships that are not just matters of *quid pro quo,* that do not fit any engineer's plan or respond to any simple conception of efficiency. It is impossible to tell what this means for the individual's sense of himself or for his outlook on the world, but we may be certain that some of our most fundamental moral ideas and some of our most deep-seated habits of feeling would be changed if we created institutions that served the other functions that families serve, but which eliminated the idea of kinship.

Tocqueville talked of the awful loneliness of individualism and democracy, which throws the individual "back forever upon himself alone and threatens in the end to confine him entirely within the solitude of his own heart." It is the family that protects most of us against this solitude and engages us, drafts us, into the sorrows and joys of our world. So long as it exists for a child or an adult, the world is not entirely impersonal, not entirely bureaucratized, at least a little individualized and personally accented. The justice appropriate to the relations between kinsmen, as Aristotle observed, is not the same as the justice appropriate to relations simply between fellow citizens. Since the time of Descartes philosophers have made the effort to build moral systems *de novo,* as though they were building geometries based on universal and abstract axioms. Perhaps the simplest reason why such efforts were bound to fail is that families exist. So long as they do exist, men cannot build up their obligations by a free act of mind or will. They do not have to *decide* to be "engaged" or "committed." They are born into a network of *prima facie* obligations, and of affections and disaffections, which are specific and concrete. They begin their moral lives *in medias res.*

This may all be rather obvious, but it helps explain, and, I think, justifies a conception that has been present in the development of contemporary welfare programs—the conception that, if it is at all possible, families should be held together, and help to children should be given within the family context. For the idea of family, of kinship, is one of the root ideas holding together and penetrating a great many of our moral ideas. And this brings us back to the radical changes in Western institutions which have made us anxious and perplexed about the future of the family.

History, pursued too far, can be an escape from a problem, not an introduction to it. I have not dwelt on the great historical trends which have affected the character and position of the modern American family in order to add my voice to the many others which proclaim that our civilization has simply taken the wrong road, and that the problems faced by contemporary families can only be solved by reversing the major directions of change that have marked the development of contemporary society. Such views are exactly analogous to complaints that the invention of the motorcar is the cause of the increase in serious traffic accidents. They confuse the context in which a problem arises with its cause, and they do not solve the problem but wash it away under a flood of empty and indignant words.

The long-range changes in social organization that have altered the nature and function of the family cannot be reversed. And just as much to the point, if they could be reversed, few of us would wish to do so. They are changes which, in their net effects, have greatly increased the freedom of choice available to individuals and have provided the setting for a new kind of human experience, an experience more various, more self-conscious, more intense. They are changes, in short, which we normally applaud and to which we are morally committed. The question is whether we can find ways to make our commitment to these changes compatible with our commitment to the ideas and institutions of kinship.

There can be little doubt, it seems to me, that this process of adaptation has hardly begun. Social attitudes that are still dominant among us with regard to the family are in the main anachronisms. It is argued, to take some conspicuous examples, that the problem of care for the aged is a private problem for individual families; that illegitimate children are a private problem; that delinquency is caused simply by the failure of parents to exercise proper authority in the home; that the decline of self-reliance, respect for motherhood, and all the other fine old values—and some of them are fine even if old—are due to the fact that we have strangely lost faith and are teaching our children the wrong things. Such arguments assume that parents are not as bewildered as their children by change; that if father is a ne'er-do-well or mother ill, there is always an uncle or aunt standing by; that authority can be exercised inside the home without regard to pressures outside the home; that self-reliance can be taught when there are no legitimate opportunities for its exercise. They make the comforting, but untrue, assumption, in short, that we still inhabit a static society of small communities and large, self-sufficient families.

Undoubtedly, the weaknesses of individuals, their ignorance, their impulsiveness, their indiscipline, help to determine where the greatest damage falls. But the problems faced by modern families are institutional in context. They arise because old imperatives that held families together have lost their force, and new supporting agencies and standards have not yet been developed to fill the gap. The preservation and strengthening of the family requires more than the attention of individuals to their family problems. It requires the strengthening of their individual capacities to do so. And it also requires organized social efforts to create an environment that is congenial to the existence of stable families.

This is a moment when the answer to any question is likely to lie in a committee report or else the magic word "research." At the risk of announcing some premature findings, without benefit of committee or prolonged research, I venture to suggest that some of the major factors behind family problems are already well known. They include inadequate schools; crowded living conditions; ill-health, physical and mental; poverty; the steady pressures, humiliations and hostilities under which racial and ethnic minorities live; the influence of a culture which makes much of technique and little of ideas and purposes; and not least, the unresolved paradoxes of a moral outlook which at one and the same time connects sex with sin, uses sex to sell its products, and teaches its young to regard a strong attraction for a person of the opposite sex as something quasi-supernatural which can conquer all and excuse all. Something has to give, and what gives, in most cases, is the individual's belief that he has been taught any standards by which he can live. I do not expect that social workers or social statesmen can produce a world in which all husbands are masterful but flexible, all wives devoted but free and equal, all parents affectionate but not overly protective, all children happy but with developing minds of their own. Even if social workers and social statesmen had much more power than they now have—and much more wisdom—they could not produce such a world. It is well to recognize that when we turn to the family we turn to the most intimate and precious area of ordinary human experience, and therefore the most perilous. And the perils are increased because our society places so large a value on individual freedom of choice and, therefore, so large a burden on individual powers of reason and self-discipline. But with all its inherent difficulties, the problem of forming and maintaining stable and vigorous families is immensely complicated by the failure to recognize that the social environment of modern families is different from that in which traditional families were sustained, and that organized and deliberate social efforts are required to provide new supports for the family.

It is also worth recognizing that such efforts are not simply attempts to shore up an old institution against the tides beating upon it. They are attempts to achieve something singular and new. For the very changes which have made the family a more precarious institution have also given us a new and immensely elevated ideal of the family. In its perfected form, it is a free relationship between a man and a woman living together and sharing common enterprises for the delight they take in one another and in mutual devotion to the good. Aristotle spoke of an ideal form of friendship, and regarded it as the principal reward of the good life, second only to the practice of philosophy itself. The modern ideal of the family is the closest approximation we have to this ancient conception. Such an ideal, no doubt, can be achieved only rarely, but its dignity remains just the same. Just to keep that ideal alive will require an effort which will be immensely costly in money, work, and lost illusions.

IV

---⟊---

The Barges on the Seine

THE CHARM OF A BARGE IS THAT IT DOESN'T TRY TO BE charming. Even in the Seine valley, it sails down its own separate thoroughfare, radiating detachment, solitude, industriousness, and the virtue of minding one's own business. Whether for this reason or some other, the barges on the Seine have had legions of admirers, and my wife and I have for some time been among them.

Last summer, knowing that I would have a few days to spare on the way home from a conference in the Soviet Union, we decided that the time had come to get a somewhat closer view of a barge than one can get from the banks of the Seine. Acting on this impulse, whose murky origins we shall leave it to others to explore, we wrote the Esso Standard Company in Paris, which operates some of the handsomest oil barges, and explained that we were admirers of barges who had never been on a barge. Whether the pathos of this appeal will work for others I can't say, but it worked for us. In what seemed like a flash, we received a courtly letter from Esso Standard's *Directeur Marine,* a gentleman with the reassuring name of B. L. Bonnefoi.

Yes, said M. Bonnefoi, Esso Standard would be glad to let us take a ride on one of its *unités fluviales*. However, M. Bonnefoi went on to say, Esso Standard's *unités fluviales* had been built for the transport of oil not passengers, and he felt that he ought to warn us that the conditions of comfort aboard "risk to appear to you mediocre." Still, if we persisted, as he put it, in our desire, Esso Standard would do all it could to cooperate. We persisted, there was a further exchange of letters with some of M. Bonnefoi's subordinates, who warned us again of the mediocrity that lay in store for us, and finally a rendezvous was arranged.

All the time that I was in Russia my interest grew in my approaching trip on a barge. Our Soviet hosts took the American delegation of which I was a member for a cruise on Lake Ladoga in a large new pleasure ship, specially chartered for the occasion, and overflowing with champagne, vodka, caviar, opera singers, balalaika players, and a jazz combo. This was followed, on the next day, and the next, by similar efforts to provide us with diversion. By the time I arrived in Paris I was ripe for proletarian pleasures, and earnestly hoping that M. Bonnefoi had meant what he said when he described the installations aboard Esso Standard's fluvial units as "mediocre."

It was not to be. My wife joined me in Paris, and we took ourselves to the quay where our barge, the *Esso Port Marly,* was tied up. Its captain, a man about fifty, short, affable, and florid-faced, came out of the wheelhouse to greet us. His name was Fulbert Hecq, and he wore well-pressed trousers, a white shirt, and a perfectly fitted blue woolen sweater. It developed that he was turning over his quarters to us. We remonstrated with him, but he was adamant, saying that he would be happy to spend the night in the crew's quarters with his sailor and mechanic, who were old friends.

Then he took us belowdecks. Our quarters consisted of a large sitting room, a dining room and a galley, complete with stove, sink, and refrigerator, a double bedroom, a single bedroom, and a washroom with shower. The walls were paneled in wood, the linoleum gleamed, the brass shone. Standing there, with the bread and cheese we had brought along for dinner hanging in string bags from our hands, we felt a little shabby.

I turned to ask the captain what could possibly be meant by "superior" facilities if these were merely "mediocre," but stopped before I got the question out. Captain Hecq was in the midst of asking my wife, a little doubtfully, whether she would truly be comfortable. When she said that she would, truly, he shrugged. "My own wife," he said, "finds that there are things that lack."

He turned and went up on deck to get us underway. It was the first but not the last time we were to discover that the people on the barges had different standards from landlocked types like ourselves.

We followed Captain Hecq to the deck and into the wheelhouse, carefully wiping our shoes, as we entered, on the mat placed just inside the door. He introduced us to his crew—Guy Cool, a sailor, a dark, solemn man in his thirties whose eyes did most of his talking for him, and Michel Deprick, a lean young man of twenty who looked more like a poet than a mechanic. The two left to cast off the lines, the motors picked up speed, and we edged away from the quay.

The *Esso Port Marly* illustrates the pregnant dictum of the eighteenth-century philosopher, Bishop Butler, to which many philosophers today are turning for solace. "A thing," said Bishop Butler, "is what it is, and not another thing." The *Esso Port Marly* is a barge. It consists of an oil tank with a small deck in front of it, and another small deck with a wheelhouse on top of it at the rear. Beneath the forward deck are the crew's quarters, beneath the rear deck the captain's. The barge is 800 tons in weight and 180 feet in length.

As a result of its dimensions, one has some peculiar sensations riding on it. Standing beside Captain Hecq at the wheel as we turned to join the traffic in the middle of the river, we watched the barge's bow, way out there, leading the way. It didn't feel as though we were on the same vessel. The bow moved and we moved, but it wasn't because the bow and stern were connected. It was merely because we were in the same gravitational field.

Eventually, however, we stopped turning, and then we seemed to feel ourselves back on the barge. One and indivisible, bow and stern set off downstream.

For a river that has played so large a part in the imagination of the Western world, the Seine is something of an anomaly. As a river, it is a bore. It does not have the majesty of young rivers that run between high palisades, nor does it have the power or drama of rivers like the Rhine or the Rhone that come down from high mountains. Between Rouen and Le Havre the waters from the sea disturb it a bit, and from time to time the Seine can give difficulty. But as far as Rouen the Seine is simply a placid, muddy, slow-moving stream of water which fades into the countryside around it, and looks as domesticated as the cows that feed along its banks. It is inconceivable that anyone could write a book about life on the Seine in which the river itself was a central, driving force, as the Mississippi is in *Huckleberry Finn*. The Seine doesn't have enough strength of character.

Indeed, the Seine is marked by its irresolution. It rambles all over the map. Bending and snaking along the Seine at twenty kilometers (twelve miles) an hour—the barge people speak in "knots" only when they get near the ocean—it took us two hours to get from Paris to the locks at Bougival. By road, Bougival is eighteen kilometers and fifteen minutes from Paris. From the point just west of Dijon in Burgundy, where the Seine originates, to Le Havre, where it empties into the sea, the distance as the crow flies is 250 miles. The distance as the Seine wanders is 500 miles. The Latin name for the river, *"Sequana,"* came, it is believed, from the Celtic word *"squan,"* which meant "tortoise."

Yet it is precisely these characteristics of the Seine, which make it physically uninteresting, that have given it its role in the history of Paris and France. It is a housebroken river. It makes a long, gentle descent to sea level. And its tortuous windings, which do not spoil it for peaceful commercial use, spoil it as an invasion route, slowing up an enemy and giving the defenders a chance to cut his lines to the rear. The King of France, seated at Paris at the center of the maze formed by the Seine, could hold off the fierce Norsemen long enough for them to be forced to settle down in Normandie and learn French, when it became possible to make a deal with them.

Indeed, the bends in the river, over the ages, have created still other advantages for a defender. The action of the waters on the concave sides of the bends has in many places created precipitous high cliffs, while, on the convex sides, debris has been thrown up by the river to create a gently sloping countryside offering broad views. The heights make ideal defense spots, where fortresses dominating the river valley can be constructed. Richard Coeur de Lion, Duke of Normandie and King of England, built such a fortress, the Château Gaillard, at Les Andelys, some sixty miles from Paris by land, at the end of the twelfth century. In doing so he reversed the traditional role of the Seine, using it not to defend Paris from the sea but to defend Normandie from Paris.

The Seine, in short, has given Paris both safety from the sea and openness to it, which may help explain both that city's openness and its quality of self-contained independence. In any event, you need be on a barge leaving Paris for only a half hour to be reminded so that you won't forget it that Paris is a seaport. For miles, as we moved downstream, the yards and docks of *Paris-Port-de-Mer* were crammed with coal, lumber, machinery, gravel, cement, and wine from North Africa, all of which had been brought up the river by barges from the sea.

Although it was August, and the traffic was only one quarter its normal amount, we were surrounded by barges the moment we left the quay. The *Esso Port Marly* rode high in the water, having just unloaded its oil. Coming at us, moving upstream, were loaded barges, their decks inches above the water. With their long snouts pushed out ahead of them and their wheel-houses standing up like little cranial bumps in the rear, they looked like dogs bravely paddling against the current, nose and eyes just above the surface. We were never out of sight of other barges all the way to Rouen. The railroads and truck routes supplement what comes to Paris on the Seine, and since the war a pipeline between Paris and Le Havre has also been built. But the Seine continues to be indispensable, offering an irreplace-ably safe and economical route for the movement of heavy car-goes.

Moreover, during the past century the channel of the Seine between Le Havre and Rouen was deepened so that ships of oceangoing tonnage could proceed to Rouen before delivering their cargoes to barges. This has enormously enhanced the Seine's usefulness. Now one can stand on a hill at Caudebec, between Le Havre and Rouen, looking out over a bucolic landscape, and watch a Soviet ship from the Baltic, crusted with salt, sail across the neat inland valley and then disappear, hidden by the poplars as it rounds a bend in the river. Paris, Rouen, and Le Havre, as Napoleon remarked, are one city, and the Seine is their street.

The Seine, indeed, is a street in more than just its abstract function. Once you are on it you find that it has traffic lights, traffic jams, and road signs—"Caution," "Dangerous Curve," "Squeeze to the Right," "Parking Permitted." And it is a street, not a turnpike. For it has a social life and an established community.

As we entered the stream of traffic on the river, Captain Hecq began to greet people, like a man out for his regular morning stroll. He waved at the occupants, it seemed, of half the barges we passed, and, invariably, they waved back at him. When we passed someone the captain knew well, he would open the door of the wheelhouse, and wave more broadly. Messages would be exchanged in sign language, the captain would laugh, and there would be answering shouts. At one point Captain Hecq waved a particularly hearty greeting to a man and woman on a barge passing us on its way upstream. "My daughter and son-in-law," he said with a smile.

The social life on the Seine has natural causes. The Seine is a street on which the life of a good part of France depends, but the people who live and work on that street form a separate, enclosed community. The captain's father and grandfather had worked on barges; so had Michel Deprick's. Guy Cool was the great-grandson of an Englishman who had married into a barge family. The children grow up on barges, and most of them, when they are not with their parents on the barges, go to a special boarding school for the children of river people and receive a special education preparing them for life on the river. When they marry, as often as not they marry into river families. In their conversation, Captain Hecq and his crew spoke of "the people of the river" and "the people of the land" as though they were two separate groups, almost two separate nations.

We stopped at the locks at Bougival to wait our turn to go through. Captain Hecq jumped ashore, and walked briskly forward to pay a call on the lockkeeper. On the barge just ahead of us, a small terrier poked his nose out the door and barked imperiously. A white-haired woman, thin and wiry, emerged, put the dog on a leash, and took him ashore. A younger woman, on the barge tied up next to us, walked forward and began to take down the clothes that had been drying on the line stretched out over the oil tank.

I noticed that all the women, young as well as old, were wearing dresses. (During the entire voyage the only slacks I saw were on the legs of the nonworking women on a British cabin cruiser, speeding up the river toward Paris.) The barges had plants in their windows, and there were curtains on the portholes of the living quarters belowdecks. In the wheelhouses, decorous children sat behind their fathers reading books.

Lucretius, recommending the wisdom of the Epicurean who has disentangled himself from the follies of the world, speaks of the "sweet" emotion one feels when one looks out to sea and sees a ship foundering, and recognizes that one is not on it. "Not that it is a pleasure and delight," he says, "that any should be afflicted, but because it is sweet to see from what evils you are yourself exempt." At Bougival, with the smell of oil in the air, the thought crossed my mind, for just a moment, that the people on the river might feel this "sweet" emotion when they looked at the people on dry land. They seemed to have found their way to reasonableness not through philosophy or self-examination but simply through the gift of a ready-made way of life.

It was after we went through the locks at Bougival that Captain Hecq began to tell us about the *pousseur*. At first, from his tone, I thought that he was talking about a strange new animal, or perhaps a river spirit, that had suddenly come to change the established life on the Seine. Then, as he continued to speak, I realized that the captain was talking about a "pusher"—a tugboat in reverse.

The *pousseur*, it appeared, had been invented in either Russia or America, or perhaps in both simultaneously—the captain was not quite sure—some half dozen years ago. Now it was being introduced on the Seine. For the economies were extraordinary. A *pousseur* worked night and day. A barge had to tie up at night. When a barge finished a trip, it had to lie over for twenty-four hours—"to get warmed up again," as the captain put it. A *pousseur* turned around and went right back.

The biggest savings were in labor. The crew of a *pousseur* consisted of three teams of four men each. Each of these teams had a ten-day rest ashore each month. The other two teams, working in alternating six-hour watches, kept the *pousseur* moving. And the *pousseur* did more than just work steadily. A *pousseur*, pushing four or even six scows or floating tanks in front of it, could move loads as high as 3,500 tons. The *Esso*

Port Marly, as self-respecting a barge as ever worked, could not move more than 800 tons.

The statistics were imposing. The barges were through. In five years all of them would be gone. The *Esso Port Marly* itself was being taken off the Seine in the fall and being sent down to Bordeaux to work on a provincial river, the Garonne. And Captain Hecq, who was moving over to the *pousseurs,* was going up to the Rhine, where the use of the *pousseurs* was already far advanced, for a two-week course of training in the use of radar.

For the *pousseurs,* the captain reminded us, raising his forefinger like a schoolteacher, the *pousseurs* work at night. And three men, working only in the day, and moving only 800 tons . . .

There was something curious about the story, and it was only after Captain Hecq returned to the statistics and began to repeat them that I realized what it was. He was repeating the statistics adoringly. He was not complaining, he was delighted. And Guy and Michel, who had entered the wheelhouse and were listening to the statistics, were nodding in admiration and approval. The atmosphere of the wheelhouse was positively electric with reverence for the *pousseur's* efficiency.

I tried to put values in their place again. "Won't many of you lose your jobs?" I asked.

"Of course," said the captain airily. "After all, three men, moving 800 tons—"

I interrupted. "But all that," I said, pointing out the window toward the barge moving alongside us, a woman and her young daughter knitting on the rear deck, "won't all that disappear?"

"Terminated," said the captain. "Finished. There is no place for families on a *pousseur.*"

I couldn't resist spelling it out, though I was a little embarrassed as the words formed themselves. "Your family traditions, the difference between the people of the river and the people of the land, your whole old way of life—all this will go, won't it?"

"Naturally," said the captain. "*Que voulez-vous?*"

We cruised along in silence for a while. Every once in a while I caught Guy Cool looking over at me to be sure I had grasped the full beauty of the story Captain Hecq had told. When I looked over at him, he would nod solemnly, like a man in church sharing with a neighbor the wisdom of the minister's sermon. Michel seemed to have been carried away by the captain's words. He had his eye on some secret and agreeable prospect all his own.

The captain began to speak again. "This is not an easy life," he said. "It is a responsibility—all this equipment, all the oil. It is on a man's mind. One has many *soucis*. Now, on the *pousseur*—" I felt my head hunching between my shoulders, but the captain did not break out into his liturgy of figures again—"on the *pousseur*," he said, "there are two captains aboard, one for each team of four men. You are captain for six hours, and then you rest. You do not have to keep worrying. On a barge it is different. You tie up at night, and you go to sleep, but only your body sleeps. Inside your *cerveau* you are awake. You must worry about the barge all night long. Your *soucis* remain in your *cerveau*."

We tied up at a parking place along the bank for the night. After dark we had the river to ourselves, except once, when floodlights lit up the water and a long double line of scows glided past. It was a *pousseur*. I had brought two small jars of pressed caviar and some vodka with me from Russia, and we asked the captain and his crew to share them with us. But their responsibilities were on their minds, and the vodka was out. They shared the caviar with us, and found the taste, they said, interesting. They turned in early, and we did too. It was wonderfully quiet. In our warm bedroom we fell asleep, not a *souci* in our *cerveaux*.

We woke early, while it was still dark, and went up on deck. The air was cool and moist, and the land, not three feet away, seemed to belong to another world. A cock crowed, and as if on signal it began to rain. It may have been the rain that changed my mood. Querulous and unworthy thoughts churned inside me. "Radar," I thought. "Day and night, and nights like days. *Pousseurs.* Pushers. Pushers and *parvenus.*"

I turned to my wife. "Eight hundred and thirty-five hundred," I said, "divided by four . . ."

"Be quiet," said my wife reasonably. "We're only passengers."

Later in the morning we stopped at the shining new locks of Notre-Dame-de-la-Garenne, and the captain went ashore to greet the lockkeeper, his son. We went ashore too to have some coffee. At the café where we sat, the cigarette butts were still on the floor, and the pinball machine stood crookedly against the wall. The bargemen had been there late the night before.

"Ask the captain," said my wife, "whether his wife ever comes with him."

I put it to the captain a little later in the morning. He looked over at my wife before he answered. "She comes with me from time to time," he said. "When she wants a change. But she prefers to stay in Rouen. She has much to do there—her house, her friends."

"And Guy," I asked, "is he married?"

"Yes," said Captain Hecq. "His family too is at Rouen."

"And Michel?" I asked.

"He is still young and a bachelor. But he has already passed his pilot's examinations. During my vacation he was captain of this barge. He makes progress, that young man."

Michel came up the ladder from his quarters forward. We walked down the narrow catwalk alongside the oil tank to join him.

"Will you go over to the *pousseurs?*" I asked.

"No," he said, "I am leaving the river."

"But you are already a pilot," I said. "Is it really so bad a life?"

Michel shrugged. "No, it isn't bad," he said. "But it's lonely, and too enclosed, and not good for the children to be so separated from others."

"But you're a bachelor, aren't you?" I asked, puzzled.

"Pour l'instant!" he replied, a little indignantly. "And the women don't like the barges, and don't like the men to be away." He stopped, and smiled at my wife. "No," he said, "that's not quite right. If you marry a woman of the river, she doesn't like the barges. But if you marry a woman of the land, often she likes the life of the river."

"Then marry a woman of the land," my wife said.

He smiled again. "That is not so easy to do," he said, "if you stay on a barge."

"What are you going to do?" I asked him.

"I'm going to be a frogman," he said. "I already have a job."

Late in the afternoon the river broadened out, and we entered the harbor of Rouen. Big ships lay at anchor ahead of us, with the Cathedral behind them. Just after we passed some docks piled high with newsprint, Captain Hecq blew the barge's whistle in four sharp blasts. On the bank to the right of us, the door of a house a few yards back from the river opened, and three children and a young woman with a child in her arms came out and ran down toward the river, waving eagerly. Guy Cool, on the deck outside, waved back. He came into the wheelhouse, smiling.

"His family," said the captain.

"How old are your children?" I asked Guy.

"One, two, three, and four," Guy said.

"He works for General de Gaulle," Captain Hecq said.

We went another quarter of a mile, and the captain blew the whistle again, this time in a complicated signal.

"My house is there on the hill," he said. "I've ordered trout for dinner."

They took us to the quay in the center of the city, just behind the bus terminal. We bade them good-by and went ashore. When we got to the boulevard that runs along the river, we turned and waved to them. They waved back. By the time we had dodged our way across the street, the *Esso Port Marly* had already turned around, and was making its way back downstream to its own berth.

The first taxi we signaled didn't stop. The driver was going too fast to see us. We got beaten out for a second taxi. On the third try, we managed to grab one. We rushed up the hill to the railroad station, and just caught the train back to Paris.

V

———❦———

The Love of Anxiety

THE PHRASES THAT AN AGE USES TO DESCRIBE ITSELF ARE NOT always the best guides to the actual character of that age. They are usually fairly good guides, however, to what that age wishes or fears it might be. Among all the labels that have been applied to the present moment in history, none, I think, has been more generally accepted than the phrase "The Age of Anxiety." And that we today have some solid reasons for anxiety can hardly be doubted. We have the old reasons that people have always had, though not so many of these reasons as our forebears had. Still, like them, we live with the certainty that we will know pain, disappointment, and death, and with the uncertainty about when or how these reminders of our mortality will strike.

In addition, we have some special reasons of our own for being anxious. The future of the race—not simply the character of that future, but whether there will be a future—is in doubt. And even if this were not the case, we should still feel that the earth was shaking underneath and the stars were no longer fixed in the firmament. The generation that is entering middle age can remember a shattering depression, a depraved political cult that fell upon an educated nation like a mad seizure, the deceptions and doctrinaire cruelties to which political utopianism has led, and a fearful war ending in a cold, precarious peace. And since the war, that generation and a rising generation have lived in a world in which the continents seem to have been cut adrift. The old comfortable balance of power between the Orient and the Occident has been destroyed. Africa and Latin America, which the West, four centuries ago, threw into a state of shock that has lasted until very recently, are now entering the mainstream of Western politics and culture and, in their turn, are upsetting the traditional foundations of Western security. And while this has been going on, a ravenous technological revolution, as far-reaching in its implications as the Agricultural Revolution or the Industrial Revolution, has been taking place. It has already changed our homes, cities, work, play, and governments, and our ideas about the uses of the moon, and we know that it has hardly begun to work its effects. Most important of all, it has immensely accelerated the pace of change itself. It is difficult to escape the feeling that even if we could find the ideas we need for living in this world and controlling it, these ideas would be outmoded by the time we found them. Anyone who thinks that anxiety is good for the human soul should be quite content with the world as it is.

But there is also another kind of anxiety from which many of us are suffering. It is a gratuitous, self-cultivated anxiety; it bespeaks a positive love of anxiety. And this cult of anxiety is the expression of a larger moral phenomenon than any that I have yet mentioned. This is the feeling, particularly widespread among those who have been initiated into the traditions of the liberal arts, sciences, and professions, that the world as it exists and as it is likely to be is not a world in which the ideals of liberal culture, or of humanity and freedom, have any significant place. It is a feeling of general alienation, of not belonging, a tired, disenchanted conviction that even if solutions could be found for our problems they would be dreary and inhuman solutions because they would have to make peace with a dreary and inhuman world.

Looking ahead to the prospects of Western civilization, Max Weber, to whom we owe so many of our ideas about modern society, expressed this sense of moral expatriation quite precisely. Either "wholly new prophets" must arise or "a powerful renaissance of old thoughts and ideals" must take place, he wrote. Otherwise we are in for it; we can expect only "mechanized petrifaction," a world of "specialists without spirit or vision and voluptuaries without heart." The fundamental imperatives of human existence in a modern, technologically organized society, it is widely felt, are such that intellect, imagination, individual personality, the intimacies of human experience, are all nuisances and are bound to be treated as nuisances. Our cities are made of cold steel and glass, and inside these transparent boxes men punch the buttons of machines and wait for the machines to give them the answers. The irreversible flow of events is simply against us.

I should like to suggest that this vague but encompassing form of anxiety is based on the wrong reasons and is directed toward the wrong things. It is an artificial anxiety, and expresses a disposition to evade dealing with the namable and locatable worries we have, because it is difficult and dangerous to deal with them, and easier to console ourselves with the thought that the heartless cosmos is ultimately to blame. Behind the phenomenon of intellectual—of studied—alienation, there are, I think, systematic intellectual reasons—half-acknowledged doctrines, explicit ideologies, rooted beliefs and disbeliefs—which manufacture insoluble dilemmas for us, and leave us pinned down in an anxiety that is a product of our own thinking. These ideas have great prestige and authority behind them. They are silently taken for granted in large sections of the intellectual world, and are shared, in a more or less diluted form, by great numbers of people, who, in this era of easy communication, live on formulas in the way in which their grandparents lived on folk wisdom. They are amalgams of beliefs about the facts, judgments about history, moral commitments, and philosophical assumptions. And they turn our minds in certain directions, leading us, I believe, to ask questions about ourselves and our situation to which only certain sorts of answers—helpless and anxious answers—can be given. Yet I do not think that most of these ideas can withstand the light of day.

Obviously, it is impossible to deal in short order with all the ideas that stand behind the contemporary cult of anxiety. Two or three of them, however, seem to me to be peculiarly decisive, and to be symptomatic of the others. These are ideas that are entertained about central features of our civilization. The first of these has to do with technology.

In his much-discussed lecture, *The Two Cultures and the Scientific Revolution,* C. P. Snow has written about the Industrial Revolution:

Almost everywhere . . . intellectual persons didn't comprehend what was happening. Certainly the writers didn't. Plenty of them shuddered away, as though the right course for a man of feeling was to contract out; some, like Ruskin and William Morris and Thoreau and Emerson and Lawrence, tried various kinds of fancies which were not in effect more than screams of horror. It is hard to think of a writer of high class who really stretched his imaginative sympathy, who could see at once the hideous back-streets, the smoking chimneys, the internal price—and also the prospects of life that were opening out for the poor, the intimations, up to now unknown except to the lucky, which were just coming within ·reach of the remaining 99 per cent of his brother men. . . . For, of course, one truth is straightforward. Industrialization is the only hope of the poor.[1]

Snow, of course, is right, if we speak very broadly. Provided we recognize that there are levels and levels of industrialization, and different approaches to it, and that the approach adopted in England, America, or Russia is not necessarily the approach to be adopted in Peru or Burma, and provided, too, that we recognize that there are political, educational, psychological, and anthropological conditions that have to be met before industrialization can take root—and these are a great many provisos—industrialization has been, and is, the only hope of the poor. It is a painful process, a traumatic one; but it has been, on the whole, an answer to a desperate problem, and not the source of the problem. Many of the complaints that were made in the nineteenth century about the process of industrialization, and many of the complaints that are made today, fail to distinguish, for example, between the misery and disorientation due to the introduction of factories and the misery and disorientation due to the sudden rise of population in the eighteenth century. The problem was akin to the problems in Asia, Africa, and Latin America today. Migrations to the cities were taking place in any case; the choice for the poor—and it is something when they have a choice—was, and is, to enter the factories or to beg on the streets.

But Snow also leaves out a great deal. He makes entering the

[1] *The Two Cultures and the Scientific Revolution* (Cambridge: Cambridge University Press, 1959).

factory look like an untroubled decision by the poor. "With singular unanimity, in any country where they had the chance," he writes, "the poor have walked off the land into the factories as fast as the factories could take them." But the poor have walked off the land, a great many of them, because they have been pushed off, because there have been too many of them, because their small plots could not support them. All over the world today, many country people, particularly the younger ones, come to the cities, to be sure, because they are attracted by the crowds, the lights, the fun, or the sin. But a great many, like the Negroes coming from the South or the Puerto Ricans from their island, come not for love of the city or of factories, but from simple desperation.

And what the poor in early industrial England found when they came to the factory towns is weakly described by Snow. He speaks of "the hideous back-streets, the smoking chimneys, the internal price." These are bland words for human excrement in the gutters; for tuberculosis; for wild bands of lost children; for the military regimen of the factories; for women doing the jobs of men; for men displaced from work, from self-respect, from their classic positions of authority. It was not Ruskin or William Morris with their nostalgic ideals of craftsmanship, but John Stuart Mill, the economist and logician, who wrote, despite all his sympathy for science and industry, that the Industrial Revolution had not improved the condition of the mass of mankind, but had made that condition worse. Snow speaks of the intellectuals as "natural Luddites," but the original Luddites, who destroyed the machines, were not writers but poor men. And a number of them suffered death for what they did.

This, indeed, is the most important thing that Snow leaves out. Industrialization was felt by the Luddites, and by the writers who screamed in horror, as a human decision. It was not just that the factories were ugly, or that the air was poisonous, or that so many of the human beings for whom industrialization, according to Snow, was the only hope, had been made so clearly wretched and hopeless by industrialization. It was that all this was done in the name of a doctrine which said that the costs should not be counted, that they were unavoidable, that all that mattered was industrialization full speed ahead, and that this was the way, the only way, to improve the race. The writers and intellectuals were opposing a gospel—the gospel, as Carlyle put it, of anarchy plus a constable—and not simply an historical process. They were opposing what we may call the doctine of the Moral Isolation of Technology—the doctrine that industrial innovation is not to be criticized, that no effort to cut the costs or to distribute them equitably should be made.

We stand in horror, and properly so, at the iron ideology which has been employed by the Russian and the Chinese leaders in this century to justify the sufferings visited on their people for the sake of industrialization. But the individuals in England and America who led the way in the industrialization of their countries, and who profited most from it, had quite similar iron ideologies. And perhaps they were right; the victory over sheer scarcity is the crucial victory, and perhaps there is no other way to win this victory than to beat and flay the poor out of their sloth and superstitions. Yet whether this is so was precisely the question they did not ask, the question which the doctrine of the Moral Isolation of Technology said could not be asked. The possibility of alternatives, not to technology but to the existing methods of introducing and managing it, was not considered.

So the critics were right in their own way, and Snow does

them less than justice. But now we must look at the critics too. For what many of them did in fact was to reassert, from their side, the same doctrine of the Moral Isolation of Technology. And this is what many of the critics of technology do today. F. R. Leavis, in his angry rejoinder to Snow, has protested that we must not regard the cultural consequences of technology as inevitable, or "acquiesce in their being accepted mechanically and unconsciously." He says of Snow: "If you insist on the need for any other kind of concern, entailing forethought, action and provision, about the human future—any other kind of misgiving—than that which talks in terms of productivity, material standards of living, hygienic and technological progress, then you are for [Snow] a Luddite."[2] But setting aside the question whether Snow has some other kind of concern (I think the evidence is that he does), what is the other kind of concern which Leavis thinks we should have? It is a concern, not with external civilization but with the individual's inner life, with his quality of awareness, with the depth and subtlety of his feelings. One thinks that one understands him and is with him. But then Leavis concludes by asking, "Who will assert that the average member of a modern society is more fully human, or more alive, than a Bushman, an Indian peasant, or a member of one of those poignantly surviving primitive peoples, with their marvelous arts and skills and vital intelligence?" And here we have the Moral Isolation of Technology all over again.

For it is only against the background of technology that the question about the humanity and the quality of consciousness of the average member of any society has been raised as a serious and practical question about the world that is here and now. It

2 *Two Cultures? The Significance of C. P. Snow* (London: Chatto & Windus, 1962).

is only in the industrialized world that the question gnaws at us, only in this world that it has been asked at all widely or insistently. Aristotle thought that some men are natural slaves; that has been the prevailing, working attitude that has governed most societies so far as the destiny of their members in this world is concerned. It is the attitude which most Indian peasants have accepted for themselves, and which many of them still accept. And this is the attitude that technology changes. It wins a victory over extreme scarcity, or promises that victory; it stirs up the envy and ambitions of the poor; it stirs the fears and the bad conscience of the rich; it tends to substitute for the old relations between the social classes, and the old ethic of deference to superiors and benevolence to inferiors, new relations based on bargaining and contracts, and a new ethic stressing equality and the equitable application of impersonal rules to all men.

Not least, technology cuts men loose from their customs and subjects them to new arrangements that are clearly human contrivances; it invites them, therefore, to distinguish themselves from the web of circumstance that surrounds them, to stand back from the arrangements under which they live and to think of alternatives. It gives more men the provocation, in a word, to distinguish between custom and reason, between mores and morals. It is an initiation, in this sense, into the reflective life, and it encourages the attitudes which make it seem so natural to ask whether there is vividness and eagerness in the lives of average people.

Leavis speaks of "the accelerating movement of external civilization . . . that is determined by advancing technology." But technology is not simply an external phenomenon which we must somehow find a way to cloak in morality and sensibility; it is an inner phenomenon, a phenomenon in the history of morality and sensibility. And its consequences are not simply to subvert morality and sensibility; its consequences, like those of any episode in the moral history of our race, are equivocal.

If we take it that technology is merely "external," and that "humanity" is internal, we may quite honestly deny being a Luddite or wishing to destroy the machines; but we are saying, in effect, that all one can do about technology is to resist and complain, that humanity and technology belong to entirely different worlds and cannot have much to do with one another. In practical effect, the attitude of the angry humanist dovetails perfectly with the attitude of the complacent engineer. The engineer says that morals are not his business; the humanist says that technology is not his. This leaves each of them with the anxious feeling that there is something important he ought to be doing which has somehow slipped his mind. On the other hand, it also leaves each free to go his own way. Anxiety is a small price to pay for this happy arrangement.

But I do not dwell on this point in order to rake over our judgments about the past. The fact is that the doctrine of the Moral Isolation of Technology is still with us. With great reluctance and after very bitter struggles, we have got used to such ideas as that there should be limits to the hours of work, or checks and balances in the economy such as those represented by collective bargaining. We also recognize that safeguards have to be erected against the dangers of technology to life and health, although the smog over London, the statistics of road accidents, and the smell of exhaust fumes in every city suggest how slow and fitful that recognition is. But on the whole we still continue to treat technological innovation as though it were a natural phenomenon like the rain. It simply comes, and the cornucopia overflows; and if by accident all this goodness happens to hurt you, there is nothing for you to do but keep out of the way. You are simply an odd fellow who is spoiling the party.

Featherbedding and the increasingly numerous work stoppages that are due to automation are symptoms of the absence of any systematic concern about the costs of technological innovation—the costs in human pride, in the forced obsolescence of human skills, in the disturbance of homes and neighborhoods—that are borne by some members of the community while others profit. In the absence of organized forethought about the social and moral consequences of technical innovation, in the absence of established procedures for distributing the costs of such innovation equitably, those who are hurt are reduced to purely defensive measures, to hostility and sheer resistance, to being contemporary Luddites.

This absence of forethought, this interest in the consequences of technology only in the realm of sheer productivity, is the consequence of the unspoken hypothesis that technological innovation is an unmixed good. That it is on the whole a good I do not dispute; but it is a mixed good. It seems to me possible to consider the consequences of innovations in the light of a broader spectrum of values than we now employ, and to bring those affected most immediately by these innovations into the circle of those who do the first thinking and planning about the conditions under which innovations will be introduced. The absence of such arrangements is one large and solid reason for anxiety and a sense of alienation.

I say, however, only that such arrangements are possible. I do not say they will be easy to create. Constellations of money, power, and interest—and, I would add, in labor as well as management—would be opposed. And more than good will, hard work, and the willingness to face some hard knocks would be required to build these arrangements. If we are prepared to try to capture our runaway technology and to bring it to heel, some rethinking of entrenched intellectual and moral positions will also have to take place. For if engineers tend to treat the social and moral disturbances brought about by technology as not quite their business, it has also to be added that few humanists have as yet taken on the task of developing the positive conceptions of the good life that are possible and appropriate for an industrial and democratic age. They guard their humanistic values as though these values would be used up if they were used. And this brings us to another doctrine which is the companion of the doctrine of the Moral Isolation of Technology. This is the doctrine of the Separation of the Sciences and the Humanities.

There was once a man who was asked if he believed in infant baptism. "Believe in it?" he said. "I've seen it!" That there is a separation, in every college and university and in society at large, between the sciences and the humanities is as plain a fact as infant baptism. The separation has existed, moveover, for centuries; and it is not simply the kind of separation that exists between a geologist and a physicist, or a student of English literature and a specialist in the Dead Sea Scrolls. It is not, that is to say, simply a difference between people whose specialties are different, and who therefore find some initial difficulty in communicating with one another. It is a separation marked by distrust and antagonism, and it is fairly intense. I do not know whether Sir Charles Snow is right in speaking of "two cultures"; but there is a conflict, and it is rather like that between two competing power blocs. And it builds into our education, and into our outlook on the world, the conviction that there is a gulf that cannot be bridged between the increasing knowledge and power that we are accumulating and the values we most cherish. The natural consequence is anxiety.

And yet, although the conflict is real enough, some fairly elementary questions about it are rarely answered clearly. What are the differences between the sciences and the humanities? Why is it so commonly taken for granted that the division between these two domains of the mind is an incurable one?

Perhaps the most common answer is that the sciences deal with nonhuman phenomena and the humanities with human phenomena. But this won't do. Psychology, sociology, and archaeology can make reasonable claims to be sciences. And if it be said that they are not really very exact sciences, then what do we do with meteorology? Darwin's theory of evolution, for all its power and epoch-making importance in the history of science, is not a highly chiseled and sharp theory; and, on the other hand, there are studies in linguistics or in the law that approach mathematics in precision.

It has been repeatedly argued, to be sure, that the difference between physical phenomena, on one side, and human behavior, on the other, is so radical that a quite different logic of inquiry is appropriate in each domain, and that it is impossible, therefore, that the study of human affairs can ever be a science. This is not the place to argue that difficult and complex question. But if "science" stands for the effort to ground opinion in evidence that is systematically gathered and evaluated and that is public in character, and if there is a difference between a disciplined study, say, of the sources of a poet's images (like John Livingston Lowes's *The Road to Xanadu*) and unfounded speculation about such sources, then there is no clear reason for asserting that "science" has no place in the study of human affairs.

Is the distinction between the sciences and the humanities, then, that the sciences are neutral with respect to values while the humanities are not? This distinction, too, turns and runs away when it is pressed. It does not apply to large areas in either domain. It is true that scientific statements are in general descriptive in character, and that it is the very essence of the scientist's business to put his preferences aside when he states the facts. But this does not mean that his statements have no implications for what are generally thought to be values. On the contrary, scientific statements have challenged religious beliefs, have revealed the superstitions on which economic systems and political programs are grounded, and have upset notions that support some of our most zealously protected moral codes. This is one reason why science so frequently arouses animosities. And, on the other hand, if there are parts of chemistry or zoology that seem to have no clear bearing on human values, the same is true for very large parts of the humanities—for example, music or the painting of Mondrian. Of course, it can be said, and truly, that these things are values in themselves or that they increase our powers of discrimination and appreciation. But precisely the same thing can be said for the pleasures that the study of science gives.

And yet these distinctions do, of course, point to some genuine and important differences between the sciences and the humanities. We think a scientist is out of character if he moralizes; we think a humanist is a pedant if he refuses to be a critic of life. We expect and want abstractions from scientists, and admire these abstractions all the more when they are very general and inclusive; in contrast, we expect and want teachers of literature to lead us back to the solidities of individual, concrete things and events. Not least, we may think a scientist's opinions are interesting, but we will not think him much of a scientist if all we hear from him is his opinions; on the other hand, we may applaud the humanist who makes an effort to support his opinions by considerations that are not matters of opinion, but we will not think him much of a humanist if there is no tough crust of personal taste apparent in him, no preferences that mark him off from others and reveal him as the special man he is. And it seems to me that these differences between the sciences and the humanities come down to two points. The first is that the sciences, including the human sciences, provide us with knowledge. In contrast, the humanities, taking literature as the prime example, provide us (among other things) with judgments. And the second point is that the notions of intellectual authority that prevail in the two domains are at odds.

These are the principal reasons, I suggest, for the suspicion between the two fields. There are other reasons too, of course. The scientists and engineers tend to earn more, they have more social power these days, they are pushing into areas such as educational planning or political moralizing where once the humanists had it all their own way. But these conflicts, when they take an intellectual form, reflect the issues that I have mentioned. And the first is that between knowledge and judgment. Humanists doubt that those with a purely scientific training, those whose heads are filled only with abstractions and statistics, are likely to deal very well with the ambiguous, emotionally charged, highly individuated situations in which men have their actual dealings with one another. They doubt, and I think they are right to doubt, that people who have never felt the diverse possibilities of life, who have never lived, even if briefly, with Macbeth's ambition or Raskolikov's crime, can have enough sense of the dimensions of human experience to be aware either of themselves or of others, or of the choices they are making for themselves and for others.

Judgment is not knowledge. It is not the ability to make abstract statements and to give objective reasons for believing these statements to be true. It is the ability to choose and to act: to distinguish the important from the unimportant, to be aware of a variety of values and to strike a balance among them, to adjust one's habits or one's ideas to the specifics in front of one. Judgment is what we expect from a judge, a gambler, a novelist, an agreeable companion. Abstract knowledge of statutes, or of the principles of probability, or of the laws of the ego and the id, or of the rules for winning friends and influencing people, are quite inadequate substitutes. They are, indeed, likely to produce doctrinaire errors unless they are used with judgment. Judgment, for that matter, is usually the extra ingredient that is responsible for important scientific work, and that distinguishes the strategies employed by first-rate scientific minds from the routine performances of the mere technicians.

Now, literature, the law, the writings of historians, are depositaries of such judgments with regard to the human scene. A humanistically oriented study of the sciences—a study which dealt with them as human achievements in a particular time and place—would reveal the sciences, similarly, to be depositaries of human judgments about the way to conduct fruitful inquiries. But this would be because the sciences were being treated as humanities. To study these humanistic fields does not guarantee you will have judgment. The humanities too, after all, can be studied pedantically and inhumanly. But to adopt a program for training people in science and technique, without exposing them to the humanistic disciplines, seems a sound approach to education only if you are eager to produce arrogant and simplistic minds. Humanists are perfectly right to think that we shall govern ourselves badly and that we shall have only truncated lives to govern if we do not keep our connections with the traditions of the humanities.

Yet judgment alone is not enough. It has its very serious limitations, and it has only been with the development of scientific institutions that the race has created a continuing protection for itself against the dangers of mere good judgment. For judgment, which is not science, is focused on the here and now; it rests on unarticulated beliefs whose boundaries are imprecise, and on funded value judgments that represent the gleanings of random experiences. Its tools are quick analogies, images, examples, precedents; it works only as long as each new situation, for all its special characteristics, is not too unlike other situations in which judgment has been employed. This is why a man with judgment about paintings may be a child in judgments about politics or education, or why men with good judgment about business or government in one country may be lamentably naïve when they turn to business or government elsewhere.

Moreover, much good judgment—and much bad judgment—prevails not because it is actually successful in practice but because it is thought to exhibit and prove the truth of conventionally accepted beliefs. It passes muster only because other people share these beliefs and act upon them too. The opposite is often true as well. The judgment works, and is sound, but quite independently of the truths it is supposed to illustrate. The platitude that is enunciated has nothing logically to do with the actions that are taken in the platitude's name. But the success of the action shores up the platitude's prestige. Think of the American economy, for example, and of the very high degree of government intervention in it, and then contemplate the repeated pronouncements on the glories of free enterprise that are made by men whose judgment is considered to be good. "There is no difficulty in deciding a case," said Lord Mansfield to a newly appointed governor of a colony who knew no law. "Only hear both sides patiently, then consider what you think justice requires, and decide accordingly; but never give your reasons, for your judgment will probably be right, but your reasons will certainly be wrong."

Judgment, perhaps worst of all, can develop its own self-protective provincialism. The man of judgment is often suspicious on principle of broad ideas, of abstractions, of systematic thinking and long-range planning. He prefers to move from situation to situation, facing each in its own terms, and moving by intuition, by common sense, by a feel for the situation; he suspects that ideas will be too simple, too bare, to deal with the complexities he actually faces. But how much does his feel for the situation leave out? Is he dealing with his problems one by one and ignoring their epidemic character? Indeed, the very idea that there were such things as epidemics eluded men of judgment for many centuries. The man of judgment has no way of checking his judgments except to use his judgment. And this will work only as long as the field in which he deploys his judgment is not changing too rapidly, or filling up too fast with unfamiliar things. For if the context in which you are making your judgments is shifting dizzily, to restrict yourself to dealing with each separate situation as it arises can be to fiddle bravely and nobly while Rome is burning.

Judgment is not a substitute, in a word, for guiding ideas or exact knowledge. Judgment, accordingly, needs to be criticized by science, which is not merely a response to experience but an effort to control experience so that it leads to ideas, and to actions through which these ideas can be refined and corrected. This, I think, is why there is hostility between the humanities and the sciences. It is not simply that the sciences are more abstract; nor is it simply that many of the sciences are more inaccessible because they employ words and intellectual machinery which ordinary people do not comprehend. These new words fix discriminations that have not been made by common sense; the intellectual machinery puts ideas in a tighter order, and allows inferences to be drawn from them that fly in the face of common sense. For some centuries now, science has been changing the world so that the old judgments do not apply; more than this, it has been invading fields where the funded judgments of the humanities once prevailed and challenging the authority of these judgments. Consider the impact of scientific knowledge on sexual morality or the invasion of politics by the methods of the pollsters, to take two elementary examples. Such events disturb the intellectual and moral peace, and it is because science is a disturber of the peace that there is much antipathy toward it, and that now, in a world in which science is making such a very large difference, we suffer from a chronic, roaming feeling of anxiety. It is for the sake of stilling this anxiety, I suspect, that we return to the idea that the humanities and the sciences are not simply separate, but that they should be separate and cannot help but be separate.

For this disturbance to our intellectual security also raises questions about our conceptions of intellectual authority. This is the second point at which the sciences and the humanities collide. The sciences aim at grounding ideas in evidence that is public in character. In the effort to formulate ideas that are susceptible to the test of such evidence, preferences are suspended, words are stripped of their agreeable overtones and associations, questions are asked that are more precise than the gross, practical questions which normally start the mind's activity. The style of science therefore clashes with many of the habits of mind that have long been installed in the humanities.

In the very simplest terms, science asks for evidence for beliefs that no one has thought of questioning before. It represents a new attitude toward received authority, and, for that matter, toward any kind of authority: it implicitly asserts that no idea or institution should have authority except in so far as it is able to stand up to continuing scrutiny. There is no way of resolving the conflict between this regulative principle and the position that the discovery and transmission of our moral heritage belongs to the humanities alone; nor can this principle, which is a principle of general intellectual discipline and not simply of science, be made compatible with the proposition that the truths pronounced by the humanities have an infallible kind of authority which makes them immune to the tests of scientific inquiry. For there are bound to be misunderstandings and conflicts between people who like to find evidence for their beliefs which they can make available to others and people who do not care for evidence or who can somehow work out definitions of evidence that invariably leave their own pet notions unscathed. Some of the first type are professional humanists; some of the second type pass as scientists. But the clash between the sciences and the humanities will remain until the morality of impersonal argument and public evidence is generally accepted in the formation of human beliefs.

So I return, by what must seem a rather circuitous route, to the love of anxiety. We have substantial causes for anxiety. But many of these genuine problems remain unmet because we blanket them in a larger, more encompassing anxiety. This is the anxiety that the cards are simply stacked against us, that the universe is such that our knowledge and our powers must inevitably be on one side and our hopes and ideals on the other. It is the anxiety of our "Age of Anxiety," the anxiety which many appear to believe is the peculiar discovery of our age, and which, certainly, many in our age appear to cultivate and to love. For it appears to be less disturbing to a great many people to believe that our civilization is split down the middle, that technology and science are in one container and humane values in another, than to explore and to try to resolve the questions that science puts to our traditional judgments and to cherished conceptions of intellectual authority.

I do not mean, of course, that the tension between science and judgment can ever be finally eliminated. I do not think it would be a good thing if it were. It is one thing to generalize. It is another to act in specific circumstances. Nor do I think that our intellectual dilemmas can all be removed by turning to "science" as the great solvent. These dilemmas are philosophical, logical, and moral. Science may help solve them, but its help is ancillary. Indeed, what it is important to see is that these dilemmas, if they can be solved, do not require to be solved by One Great Solution. They need to be solved only where specific conflicts appear. To do so, however, requires a general disposition to question and analyze, and a rejection of the principle that our intellectual and moral lives are divided down the middle, with science and machinery on one side and humanity and the good life on the other.

A general disposition to question and to analyze will of

course produce its own anxieties. Unquestionably, men run perils, internal and external, when they refuse to recognize that any human beliefs or practices, including their own, occupy a safe realm protected from rational scrutiny. It is a refusal that has generated and will always generate considerable anxiety. But men run perils that are at least as great when they do not have this disposition to question and analyze, and greater perils still when they argue themselves into the fallacious belief that some of their most cherished ideas and values are immune to inquiry. A willingness to follow the argument wherever it leads produces a kind of anxiety that is more specific, more manageable, and more productive than cosmic anxiety. And, in any case, it is the kind of anxiety with which a civilized mind deliberately chooses to live.

VI

The Bear and the Beaver

ONCE THERE WAS A BEAR WHO LIVED IN THE WOODS. HE USED TO spend most of his time on vacation. He went on vacation during the spring, summer, and fall, and then in the winter he went to his cave and hibernated.

When he hibernated he just slept. He used to sleep three or four months at a time. Then, when he got through hibernating, he would go on vacation again.

Late one fall he was beginning to get sleepy—that is, sleepier than he usually was—and he was thinking about hibernating. He was walking along by a stream, and he happened to run into a beaver.

This beaver was very busy carrying sticks in his mouth—so busy that he didn't see the bear coming along. And the bear was thinking about hibernating, so he wasn't noticing very much either, and that's how they ran into each other.

When they ran into each other the beaver came up with a thud and dropped his sticks, and the bear said to the beaver, "For goodness' sake, will you please take it easy," and the beaver said, "For goodness' sake, I can't, I'm too busy."

"Doing what?" asked the bear.

"I'm busy working," said the beaver. Then he looked at the bear and said, "Don't you ever work?"

"No," answered the bear, "not that I know of."

"Don't you want to make anything of yourself?" asked the beaver.

"What do you mean," said the bear, "make anything of yourself?"

"Not myself," said the beaver a little crossly, "yourself. We're talking about you."

"Me?" said the bear.

"Yes, you," the beaver said. "Don't you want to get ahead in life?"

"What do you mean, ahead in life?" the bear asked.

"Well, you know," the beaver said, "well placed . . . safe . . . so you know where your next meal's coming from . . . important."

"Oh," the bear said.

"That isn't a very good answer," said the beaver. He looked at the bear for a moment. "You know you can't get any place unless you work and plan and save," he said.

"Don't you ever sleep?" asked the bear.

"Of course I sleep," the beaver answered. "On a regular schedule."

"And do you eat?"

"Of course I eat," the beaver said. "I have fixed things so that I know exactly where my next meal is coming from. And believe me," said the beaver, "that's a great comfort in this life." The beaver looked up at the bear. "You know something?" he said.

"No—what," said the bear.

"I think," said the beaver, "that it would do you a lot of good to learn how we beavers live. It would teach you something."

"Do I want to learn something?" asked the bear.

"Of course you do," the beaver said. "My goodness, if you don't, what will you ever learn?"

"Well," said the bear, "we bears are noted for our open minds, so I will try your way of life if you will try mine."

"Fine," said the beaver. Then he looked up at the bear. "What?" he asked. "Try yours?"

"If it wouldn't be too much trouble," the bear said. "I'd appreciate it."

"What would I have to do?" asked the beaver.

"You'd have to hibernate," said the bear.

"Hibernate?" asked the beaver.

"Yes," said the bear. "It's a little like sleeping—only more so."

"Well," said the beaver, "I don't know."

"I wish you would," the bear said. "I have a cave, and I hate to see it go to waste."

"All right," said the beaver, "it sounds only fair."

"My cave's up in the hills," said the bear. "Go up to the big boulder, make a sharp left turn, follow your nose, and you're there."

"Well, all right," said the beaver. He looked around. "You won't forget to take care of things now, will you?"

"Sure," said the bear. "I mean I won't."

"I hope not," said the beaver. He put his sticks down in front of the bear. "I'll leave these with you," he said, and turned to go. "You said sharp left at the boulder?" he asked.

"That's right," said the bear. "You can't miss it."

"All right," said the beaver, "so long." And he started off toward the hills.

"So long," said the bear. "If you want anything to eat you'll find a lot of stuff just hanging around. Good hibernating."

After the beaver went away, the bear sat down on the dam and looked at the fish in the pool. "Well, this is really something," he said to himself. "All these fish swimming around in the pool and they can't even get by the dam. That beaver certainly has things well arranged. I think I'll have a bite to eat." So he dipped his paw into the stream and pulled out a couple of fish and had lunch.

After lunch the bear felt very sleepy, and he was just about to fall asleep when it began to rain. "Oh, well," said the bear, "I'll go on over to that big willow tree on the bank and get myself comfortable and keep dry." So he walked to the willow tree and lay down.

He was just about to fall asleep again when he noticed something. Three or four little sticks that had been in the dam had been washed away by the rain so that now there was a hole in the dam and the water was leaking through. "I guess I'd better fix that hole before I take my nap," said the bear. So he got some twigs and put them in his mouth and carried them out to the dam.

But suddenly there was a sharp flash of lightning and a loud crack of thunder and it began to pour.

The bear looked up. "It's raining," he said.

The bear got very wet very fast, and the water in the stream got higher and higher and came faster and faster. The bear almost got washed off the dam because the water was coming so fast. Very quickly, he grabbed onto the dam with his teeth. And when he did, all the twigs fell out of his mouth.

Oh, dear, thought the bear, I came out here to fix this hole in the dam, and now I've lost all the sticks that I was going to use for fixing it. As a matter of fact, I'm having a lot of trouble just staying on this dam at all. I think I'd better get back under that willow tree.

So he tried to get off the dam. But the water came faster and faster, and things got wetter and wetter, and the dam kept getting weaker and weaker. There was so much water that the water broke through the dam and the dam washed away. The bear fell into the water.

"Oh, well," he said, "I was getting wet anyway."

With great difficulty he climbed out of the stream and got back under the willow tree. But he had to keep walking back and forth because he was so cold.

Meanwhile the beaver had arrived at the bear's cave. "Now I wonder," he said to himself, "what I have to do to start hibernating," and he looked around the cave. It was warm and dry. "Why, nothing," he said to himself a little sleepily, "nothing at all. I don't have to do anything to hibernate but just lie down." So he started to hibernate.

After a while it stopped raining at the stream. The bear looked out, and he said to himself, "I'm hungry." He was really a lot hungrier than he'd been in a long time because he hadn't had so much exercise in a long time. But he wasn't worried. The way the beaver has things arranged, he thought, there must be fish in the pool.

The bear went to the wrecked dam but there weren't any fish. There wasn't any pool either, for that matter. Oh, well, thought the bear, there must be fish somewhere around here. He started to walk down the stream and took a few steps and then suddenly he remembered. "Oh, dear," he said, "I'd forgotten that I promised to watch the dam. I'd better fix it," and he went back and started to fix the dam.

First he took all the twigs that were lying around on the bank and knitted them together. Then he got some big logs, and after much shoving and dragging and hauling and toting he pushed the logs into the middle of the stream. Then he took the twigs and put them on top of the logs. He saw that he didn't have enough twigs, so he went into the woods and cut some more sticks with his teeth and brought them back to the stream and wove them together and placed them on top of the other twigs. Then he got mud and put it in between the sticks and twigs.

He worked this way all afternoon and by the time evening came he had finished making a new dam. He would have been pleased with himself except that by this time he was very hungry. He sat on the dam in the dark and waited until some fish came along, and he caught them and had his supper. Then he was quite sleepy from all the work he had done, so he fell asleep.

But the bear had great difficulty sleeping. He kept tossing and turning and thinking about all the things he had to do. After a little while he got tired of tossing and turning, and stood up and said, "I think I ought to do some work. I'd better get some extra sticks and twigs and pile them up here and have them ready in case of emergency."

So the bear went off into the woods and cut twigs and sticks and brought them to the side of the stream and piled them up neatly. By the time he was through it was morning. So he went out to the dam where he found some fish swimming in the pool and had them for breakfast.

When he finished breakfast he looked down at the dam. If this dam were a little bigger and a little thicker, he thought, then it would have to rain a lot harder for it to be washed away. I think I'll make it a bit bigger and thicker. Then he went and got all the twigs and sticks he had piled up the night before and carried them out to the dam, and made the dam bigger and thicker.

But then he found that he didn't have any more sticks and

twigs for his reserve pile because he had used them up making his dam bigger, so he had to go into the woods to get some more sticks and twigs. After he brought them back, he piled them up neatly and made a new reserve pile.

The bear was working so hard that he almost forgot to have his lunch. But on one of his trips out to the dam he happened to notice a couple of fish in the water, so he stopped and had a quick snack.

"You know," he said as he finished, "there's one thing about this life—everything is very convenient. You can certainly eat fast. It's a lucky thing I thought to have this dam here, because if I hadn't it might have taken me a couple of hours just to have lunch. There's certainly one thing you have to realize, and that is that you can't just eat for pleasure."

So the bear spent the winter working like a beaver.

Sometimes it rained or snowed very hard, and then the bear had to work quite fast to keep his dam from breaking. And when it was good weather he worked even harder because he had to take advantage of the good weather to do all the things he couldn't do in the bad weather. "One thing I've learned," he used to say to himself, "if you don't work you don't eat."

Once it was sunny for a whole week. And the bear got an idea.

He thought that if he built a second dam a little farther down the stream, then if the first dam broke it wouldn't be so bad because he'd have something to fall back on. So he spent the week of good weather building a second dam. And when he was through he had to go into the woods and cut a lot more sticks and twigs to build himself a second reserve pile.

Now when it rained the bear had to work much harder than before because he had two dams to keep from breaking. He was always running back and forth from one to the other. Nevertheless, he felt much safer that way. I'm planning ahead, he used to think, as he ran from one dam to the other.

By the end of the winter the bear had everything all worked out. He ate twice a day, ten minutes for breakfast and fifteen minutes for dinner. In the evening he would knit twigs for an hour. And he made sure to get eight hours' sleep every night, no more no less. "I absolutely can't do with less," he would say, "and I certainly can't afford more."

He got to look very much thinner and his eyes were usually rather red, but the bear didn't mind. He was on the move pretty much all the time, so he felt that it was a good thing that he had less weight to carry around. And he didn't know that his eyes were red because he never stopped to look at himself.

As the bear used to say, "That's one advantage to this life. You're so busy you don't have time to worry about how you feel."

One day in the spring the beaver came back to the dam. He came through the woods humming quietly to himself, and once, when a butterfly landed on his nose, he looked at the butterfly and the butterfly looked at him, and they didn't do anything else for about an hour.

After the butterfly flew away, the beaver took a short nap, and then stood up and started to walk again, though he stopped once to cut a spring blossom. Finally, holding the blossom in his paw, he came out on the bank of the stream and saw the bear. But the bear was so busy working that he didn't see the beaver.

"Hello," said the beaver, "how are you doing?"

But the bear was so busy he didn't hear the beaver.

"Hey!" called the beaver, but the bear kept right on working and still didn't answer. So the beaver took his large flat tail and he slapped the water hard five times, which is the way beavers get attention. But the bear didn't even look up from his work.

So the beaver backed up to the bear and slapped the bear on his tail. "Ouch!" said the bear, and he dropped his sticks and looked up. "What did you have to do that for?" said the bear. "Especially when I'm working."

"Well, for goodness' sake," said the beaver, "will you stop working for a minute?"

"I can't," said the bear. "I'm too busy."

"Doing what?" said the beaver.

"Doing my work," the bear said. "You see, I just have to finish fixing this dam today, because tomorrow I have to see that both my reserve piles are all right, because Wednesday I'm planning to build a catwalk between the two dams I have now so I can run between them faster, and I really don't have much time to lose. Anyway, it might rain."

"Oh," said the beaver.

"You see what I've been doing?" said the bear, leading the way out on the dam.

"I don't have to," said the beaver. "I can guess."

The bear pointed into the water. "That's one of the best things you had around here," he said, "storing up fish in this pool. It makes things very convenient."

"Fish?" asked the beaver, who wasn't really paying attention very closely.

"That's right," said the bear. "Fish. You know—for eating."

"Oh," said the beaver, "you eat fish?"

"Of course I eat fish," said the bear. "You have to eat something."

"I used to do it a little differently myself," the beaver said. "I used to eat bark."

"Bark?" said the bear. "You mean the bark from those branches?" He pointed to the sticks in the dam.

"That's right," said the beaver. "That way you can eat while you're working."

"Bark!" said the bear. "How did you ever think of that?"

"I don't know," said the beaver. "I suppose it just came to me."

"Bark!" said the bear. "I never thought of that."

"It saves time . . . or something," the beaver said.

"And you need all the time you can get on this job," said the bear.

"I suppose so," the beaver said, yawning a little.

"You know," the bear said, "there's one thing I've learned, and that is if you don't work you don't eat."

"You've got that wrong," said the beaver. "If you don't work you don't eat—if you're a beaver."

"That's right," said the bear, "if you're a beaver." And he bent down to fix a broken twig in the dam.

Then he straightened up and looked at the beaver. "If you're a beaver!" he said.

The bear turned and put down his sticks. "Do you know," he said, "I think I'll go back and be a bear." And he walked off the dam and started back toward the hills.

The beaver looked at the stream, and the two dams, and the two reserve piles. Then he turned and looked at the bear on his way to the hills. "If you don't mind," he called, "I think I'll go back and be a bear too."

VII

The Awful Idea of Being an Individual

NO DOUBT IT IS MERELY OBSTINACY ON MY PART THAT LEADS ME to ignore the standard approach to the theme that is about to occupy us. That theme is the nature, responsibilities, and prospects of the individual. The standard approach to this theme is to begin by announcing that the individual is in serious trouble. He has been uprooted by modern society, and debauched by modern culture; he has been softened by the modern State, and turned into an automaton by modern industry; he is loaded with responsibilities by modern democracy which he is incapable of bearing; and, as if all this were not enough, an international conspiracy is out to get him.

Having thus cheered everyone up, the standard approach goes on to place the blame for this state of affairs. Without fear or favor, it names the culprit. He is the individual. Conformist yet self-centered, alienated yet mindlessly absorbed in his materialistic pursuits, the individual sits by passively, so the story goes, refusing to accept his responsibility for the condition of the world. Then, having named the disease and identified the cause, the standard approach moves serenely to its conclusion. What is the purpose of all our blood, sweat, and tears? What is the *raison d'être* for our economic system, our foreign policy, our hydrogen bombs? It is the preservation of the individual—this creature whose efficiency and intelligence, whose happy life and attractiveness and courage, the standard approach has been celebrating so persuasively.

I hope a kind interpretation will be placed on my decision not to employ this approach in discussing the individual and his prospects. It is not that I am unaware of its charms. The standard approach would allow me to demonstrate that I am not complacent, that I seek radical cures for radical disorders, and that, when the chips are down, I will not be stopped by respect for logic from stating on just which side of the fence I stand. Still, I am prepared to give up these advantages for the sake of discussing the much-mooted question of the individual in the modern world in what I think are more fruitful terms. Let us neither bury the individual nor praise him. Let us ask who he is, and why he should be alternately pitied as a victim of modern life, condemned as the source of our troubles, and glorified as the summit of creation.

It will help us to look at the question freshly, I think, if we start by noticing some of the ways in which we employ the concept of individuality.

Perhaps the first and simplest way is when we speak of "an individual" in the straightforward numerical sense of the term. This match and this match and this match are each individual matches, because each can be separately counted, and because, when counted, each adds the number 1 to the sum. And it is simply one of the characteristics of our ordinary experience that some things are identifiably separate from other things, and therefore separately countable, and that some things are not.

Thus, if you are asked to count the stars in the sky, you will know what is meant even though you may find that there are too many stars to count. But if you are asked to count the skies, you will merely be puzzled. You can count the drops of water falling from an eyedropper into a glass, but you cannot count the water in the glass. You can count the grains of sand in the desert, but you cannot count the heat you feel, though it is palpable and measurable. And most pertinent to our subject, you can count human beings. They come in physically separate bodies. No doubt, this is hardly arresting news. But if our world did not contain human individuals in this rudimentary sense of the term, we should certainly not be as concerned as we are about the moral and political ideal of individuality.

Still, this is, of course, only the barest beginning of what we mean when we speak of "an individual." Numerical individuality is not what we are talking about when we praise or condemn "the individual" or worry about the future of individualism. Slave traders no doubt counted their individual slaves; this did not mean that they recognized that their slaves were individuals. We also mean something else by "an individual." I shall call this the comparative meaning of the term.

Take two separate individuals, and one will be blond and the other red-haired, one will be thin, the other fat. It is a common fact of life that individuals, numerically speaking, are also different, qualitatively speaking. Compared to one another, each is singular not only because each counts for one but because each is odd. This is the second common way in which we use the term "individual." We use it when we wish to point to the fact that a man has special characteristics when compared to another man, or to other members of the group, or to a presumed average.

But now we come to those aspects of the idea of an individual which make it an idea that contains much more than meets the casual eye. For when we compare one thing to another, and decide, as a consequence, that we have an individual in front of us, we make this comparison only between things that seem to us to bear certain important resemblances to each other too. If we compared a man to a dog, for example, and called the man an individual because he refused to bark at the sight of a bone, this would call attention to our own singularity, not to his. On the other hand, when we compare two men and one barks at bones, he has shown a strikingly individual characteristic. In short, the idea of an individual is tacitly correlated, generally, to the idea of a type or a class.

Equally important, our recognition of individuals is also correlated to our notions of what is important—what makes a difference from the point of view of our practical, moral, or intellectual values. After all, if you take any two things, it is always possible to show that there is some respect in which they are alike and another respect in which they are different. Cabbages and kings both have circulatory systems; this blue-eyed, blond child is fifteen minutes younger than his blue-eyed, blond identical twin. The heart of the issue lies in what we consider a significant difference. This regular fellow, who perfectly echoes the opinions of all regular fellows and perfectly copies their dress and deportment, is no doubt at the same time one more little echo, one more perfect Xeroxed copy. He is, therefore, unquestionably an individual, numerically speaking. And since being an individual is highly regarded in all the best circles these days, he may put in a claim to be an individual in comparative terms as well, offering as evidence the fact that he has a wife named Isolde, a distinction that no other regular fellow shares. It is doubtful, however, that any of us would honor his claim to be an individual for this reason alone.

In speaking of individuals, in sum, a great deal normally depends on the particular system of classification and the particular scheme of values we choose to employ. And this brings us to the full-fledged use of the term "individual," to what is involved when we speak of "*the* individual" and of individualism. This might be called the systematic use of the term. If we want to know what we mean by an "individual" in other than a bare numerical sense, and in other than the simplest comparative sense, we must look not only to simple, observable physical facts but to something a little less innocent and a little more complex. We must look to a system of definitions and guiding principles. For what is individual, logically speaking, is opposed to what is general or universal. The specification of individuality, if it is more than mere numerical individuality, *is always relative to some particular system of general ideas.*

I do not make this point simply for its intrinsic interest. There is a moral to it. There is much talk these days, and much debate, about "creativity" and "conformity," about the respective merits of "self-expression" and "discipline," about the conflict between the demand for equality, on one side, and the rights of the individual, on the other. A good deal of this talk, on both sides of the fence, strikes me as vapid. For it makes very little sense, it conveys no information but only a conviction of piety, to speak of "the individual" *in vacuo.* To say that a man is an individual is to say that in some respects he does not fit the rules. But this tells us little about him unless we know what rules he does not fit; and it does not tell us what to think of his individuality, or whether to applaud or condemn it, unless we know what to think of these rules.

Thus, despite a good deal of sentimentality on the subject, "dissent" is not the name of an unqualified virtue. Dissent is a useful and necessary phase of inquiry, of social reform, and of the discovery of one's own individuality. Certainly, when there is nothing to be said for a belief except that it is generally believed, and nothing to be said for doing something except that the crowd is doing it, there are good reasons, judging from the experience of our species, to suspect that the belief is false and the practice discreditable. And yet there is no wholesale case for being a dissenter. Assent, not dissent, is the desirable action when the propositions before the mind are true, or the moral proposals under consideration good. Everything depends, in a word, on what the dissenter dissents from.

We come, then, to the heart of our question. Granted that we cannot understand what is meant by "an individual" in the systematic sense of the term unless we know the rules and values to which the idea is correlated, what, then, are the rules and values that give meaning to the special concept of "the individual" that has characterized Western society and the Western moral outlook—or has been said to characterize that society and outlook—in the modern world? For when we today speak of "*the* individual" we are not speaking of any old individual, but of a special type of man and a peculiar ideal of life; and not all individuals belong to this type, and fewer still exemplify the ideal.

The concept of the individual, as we have come to know and use it, is the product of a gigantic historical process of social disengagement. In this process, which has taken many centuries, and which is still going on—the process has only begun in many parts of the world—it came to be denied that the identity of any man could be fixed, or his rights and responsibilities assigned, simply in terms of his membership in any social group or any congeries of such groups. Family, village, craft, class, church, and sex, it came to be believed, told men something about who people were, and what their rights and opportunities should be; but these classifications did not tell everything. Men and women were no longer conceived as finding their *raison d'être* wholly as parts of the social procession, or merely as links in the great chain of mutual services and obligations. The doctrine of individualism came to insist, on the contrary, that their identities were more than could be fixed by any card of identity, more than could be caught by any system of classification. And the object of individualism as a social movement was to release men from irrevocable subservience to any group, and to give them some choice about their associations and obligations.

The concept of the individual, as it emerged in the modern world, thus denied principles for the governance of man that had long been accepted. It expressed a series of radical renunciations. The tests of pastoral approval or ancient authority were rejected in intellectual matters; established convention was declared irrelevant in the arts; birth and inherited privilege, it came to be thought, should no longer carry an immediate sanction in society; commands imposed from the outside came to be regarded as a very poor foundation for morality. And implicit in these rejections and denials, of course, there was a positive idea and ideal. It was the concept of the free, mobile individual, moving around from place to place, moving up or down in society as he had the chance, and retaining, as the one continuing thread of personal identity, through all these changes and choices, his judging mind, his feeling heart, his personal conscience—the judging mind of Descartes, the feeling heart of Rousseau, the personal conscience of Kant.

It is the ideal of an individual for whom the fundamental and continuing experience of life is the experience of choice, and of personal responsibility for one's choices. Individualism as an ideal, indeed, does not, when thoroughly understood, promise anything particularly comforting, like pleasure or happiness. It does not guarantee either pleasure or happiness as a reward for being an individual. It promises, for better and often for worse, only a heightened consciousness of one's own existence and character—only an intensification of experience, whatever the experience is.

The concept of *the* individual, then, is the concept not simply of numerical individuals but of individuals freed from any foreordained place or rank, and carrying with them fundamental guarantees of liberty and security, no matter where they are or with whom they deal. And the scheme of values on which this concept turns is a radically new one as the history of mankind goes. For the words that go with the concept of the individual are words like "doubt," "decision," and "choice." Above all, choice. Men discover their individual identities when they make a break with what they have been told, when they decide, despite the group, to go it alone. And if "doubt," "decision," and "choice" strike us as names for a miserable condition of life, then so much the worse for us. For there is no getting around the fact that the thought of being an individual, when its full force dawns on one, is a rather formidable and frightening thought.

What are the prospects of this ideal of the individual? What are the prospects for preserving and producing people who rather enjoy the awful idea of being an individual? I do not have a crystal ball. The future of the individual depends on many different things. I would say, however, that among these many things three seem to me peculiarly decisive. The first is a proper estimate of the meaning of contemporary tendencies of change in industry, government, science, and administration. The second is the development of a morality relevant to the special contexts that have been created in our society for individual behavior. And the third is the degree to which we can learn to make our peace with the idea of individuality, and properly to appraise the responsibilities that go with it.

As to the significance of contemporary changes, it is very commonly believed that the growth of our society, the organization of work around assembly lines and inside bureaucracies, the advent of the mass media, and the leveling effects, so called, of democratic institutions and the Welfare State, have all condemned the individual to a relatively quick, though not quite painless, death. With respect to these tendencies, I would not say, with the infant bug in *Pogo* who ran for President, that everything is just fine. But apocalyptic views concerning the inevitable consequences of these tendencies are not justified. Specialization, cities, the growth of skills, the higher levels of education needed in modern societies, the opening of opportunities and, lest it be forgotten, the replacement of routine work by machines provide conditions for the larger realization of individuality if we wish to use them in that way. There is no guarantee that we will; but those who mourn the inevitable death of the individual, it seems to me, are often merely complaining that the burdens that go with being an individual —the doubts, the choices, the work, the need for imagination— are very great. That is true enough, but individuals have never been made except by bearing these burdens.

A willingness to bear such burdens, however, is naturally dependent on a conception of what these burdens are. And it is true that the context for action by individuals today has largely changed. Increasingly, the man who would make a difference in the world has to work through large organizations, bureaucratically organized. In such organizations it is sometimes hard to recognize one's own contribution; and it is enormously difficult to move such organizations, to produce changes in them against the sheer force of their inertia. Most difficult and troublesome of all, when a man works in a large organization he is under dual directives. He has a responsibility to live by the bureaucratic discipline, to respect the organization's rules or the society's reasons for having him in the position he fills; but he also has a responsibility to look beyond his position, to take the measure of what he is doing, and to think and judge for himself. The proper balancing of these dual claims upon the individual is the recurrent, and perhaps most characteristic, moral problem of our day.

In facing this problem, however, it will help to recognize that there is almost certainly no formula that will solve it in a wholesale way. The recognition that it exists, the awareness on the part of the individual in a large organization that there are, after all, two sides to his obligations, is, indeed, a very large part of what is needed to deal with it. Moreover, in its essentials, the problem, it seems to me, is simply part of a difficult process of education in which the Western community has been engaged for some centuries. It is continuous with the problem of transforming the character of moral reflection and moral imagination that has been with us since the advent of the ideal of the free, mobile individual.

Individualism registers the fact that relations between people have become fluid and subject to change. It registers the fact that the loyalties and obligations of human beings, because the ties of kinship, neighborhood, and personal association are all looser, are likely to be more impersonal, more abstract. And in consequence, in place of the particular loyalties and the string of personal obligations that constitute morality in traditional societies, it substitutes a critical and reflective morality, appealing to abstract principles like conscience, to general standards like utility, to disinterested and universally oriented feelings like the sentiment of humanity. The problem of bureaucratic morality is a part and product of such developments, and has to be solved in such terms. And it is because, in general, the moral problems of an individualistic social order are problems of this abstract sort that so heavy a burden falls on our capacities to educate and to communicate. Men are not likely to recognize their responsibilities immediately or intuitively in a world like ours. These responsibilities need to be dramatized for the most conscientious of us, and they need to be analyzed and weighed if we can make any claim to conscientiousness at all.

But what are these responsibilities—the responsibilities that go with individuality? Obviously, there is no official, unchanging list. But certain responsibilities do appear to be basic and to provide a cue to the rest. One, a prerequisite to all the others, is the responsibility to respect the rights, the individuality, of others. A second is to recognize, as we have come increasingly to recognize over the past generation, that there is a great difference between an abstract right to be free and individual and the effective power to exercise that right. It is one thing to have a legal right to work, think, or live as one wishes. It is another thing to have the resources, the information, the associations and the education to do so. An active regard for the rights of others, a concern that these rights be used and enjoyed, entails a concern to create conditions in which these others have the opportunity to be themselves and to choose their way of life. Individualism, in a word, needs conscious social organization and support—the provision of education, the creation of diverse opportunities, and the provision of the elementary economic securities requisite for the fulfillment of the individual's design of life. It is a mistake to imagine, in fact, that classic individualism denied the dependence of the free individual on social groups; it merely opposed his being irrevocably bound down to any group. We lean on one another, we have always leaned on one another, whether we are individuals or not.

Individualism, indeed, has always been associated with the ideal of equality of opportunity. Opportunity to do what? In the end, there is only one fundamental opportunity that seems to me to matter; all other opportunities are merely conditions for it. It is the opportunity to live the kind of life one wants. But this opportunity is not something that is simply given to most men. It has to be created for them. Once they have it, they may misuse it or ignore it. That is their business. But doubts about the validity of individualism as a moral ideal, doubts that most men will know what to do with it or that they really want it, are, to say the least, premature. Most men have not yet had a chance to try individualism under circumstances that might constitute a fair test.

VIII

———◆———

George Santayana:
Solitude and Sincerity in Philosophy

GEORGE SANTAYANA IS THE MOST ACCOMPLISHED WRITER IN philosophy America has possessed. America, however, never quite possessed Santayana, and American philosophers still do not know what to do with or about him. He thought Boston, where he grew up and was educated, "a moral and intellectual nursery, always busy applying first principles to trifles." He thought Harvard, where he taught philosophy for more than twenty years, a place of "generous intellectual sincerity," but of "such spiritual penury and moral confusion as to offer nothing but a lottery ticket or a chance at the grab-bag to the orphan mind." And he thought America, even sixty years ago, only too much the land of "that 'producer's economy' . . . which first creates articles and then attempts to create a demand for them; an economy that has flooded the country with breakfast foods, shaving soaps, poets, and professors of philosophy."

As soon as he prudently could, Santayana gave up being a professor of philosophy and left the United States. The last half of his life he spent in Europe; but while he carried a Spanish passport, he continued to write in English. And, though he moved among Europeans, it was mainly in America that he was read, and it is almost entirely in America that he is actively remembered today. Even here, despite the fact that his novel, *The Last Puritan,* and the first volume of his autobiography were both best sellers when they appeared, he is remembered mainly by professors of philosophy—and by a decreasing number of them.

Yet to turn to almost any one of his books again is to be reminded of his extraordinary powers—the glinting prose, the suave, seductive dialectic, the cool majesty of his judgments and their emotional and imaginative range, the tough, unbending spine of personal taste and unembarrassed personal predilection which is always present in his judgments and which saves them from a vacant impartiality. And these books also remind us of the fascinating puzzle which Santayana as a man represents, and which his ideas represent in the history of American thought and the history of philosophy.

If it is hard to locate him as a thinker belonging to any specific country, it is even harder to fix his place in the movement of philosophic ideas or the debates between philosophical schools. He eludes professorial categories. How can you classify and be done with a man who declared that there is no God but that Mary is His mother? Santayana was a materialist and also a Platonist, a skeptic and yet a spokesman for what he called "animal faith," an unworried unbeliever whose strongest moral sympathies were aroused by religion, and by Roman Catholicism among all religions. Equally important, the professors find it hard to take seriously a man who did not take them seriously—who stood apart from all the controversies, and scoffed at his colleagues' little efforts to be original.

In his history of philosophy, Bertrand Russell (whom no one has ever accused of excessive pedantry) says nothing about Santayana, although he knew him personally and had often discussed philosophy with him. When asked his reason for the omission by one of Santayana's friends, he replied that there was nothing original in Santayana's philosophy; all came from Plato and Leibniz. But, as Santayana remarked, this judgment showed that Russell was considering him as a logician only, and ignoring the more important things about him. The last thing he wished to be as a philosopher, he once observed, was original; he preferred to speak for "human sanity," for "human orthodoxy." "Here is one more system of philosophy," the preface to his major treatise in systematic philosophy, *Realms of Being*, begins. "If the reader is tempted to smile, I can assure him that I smile with him, and that [in] my system . . . I am merely attempting to express for the reader the principles to which he appeals when he smiles."

If Russell thought that Santayana had made no contribution to the history of philosophy, Santayana thought, in effect, that Russell was too concerned to make a contribution to the history of philosophy, to the record of man's changing views—and too unconcerned with those aspects of philosophy and of human experience that transcend sectarian controversy or fashions in thought. Basically, he regarded Russell as a genius who had wasted his talents chasing one intellectual scent and social cause after another. His remark about Russell's *Inquiry into Meaning and Truth* is symptomatic: "It is not first-class philosophic writing, but only interesting current controversy. . . . He is now old enough to settle his accounts and give us his testament."

Russell's verdict—or, rather, the approach to philosophy which that verdict symbolizes—has to a considerable extent en-

gulfed Santayana. Philosophers in England and America have
become more preoccupied than they were even in Santayana's
day with the analysis of language and with problems in the
theory of knowledge. Moreover, they are spending their time
(again, even more than in Santayana's day) taking in one another's intellectual laundry—simply criticizing one another's
views, that is to say, and treating philosophy as a dialogue between philosophers unbroken by reference to anything outside
philosophy. This is bound to thrust into the shadows the view
of a man who looked upon philosophy as an effort to appraise
the vital experience of mankind in the light of rational ideals.
Santayana was a detached man—in heritage, by temperament,
by choice. He enjoyed his uselessness to the busy world. Yet he
thought that philosophy loses its moorings when it ceases to be a
commentary on the active career of mankind in the natural
world and in the worlds of mankind's imaginings.

Santayana held a conception of philosophy, in fact, that was
simple, classic, and fresh. He conceived philosophy as a man's
attempt to know where he stood. "What you need," he wrote a
young man who had urged him to give up metaphysics for literary criticism, "is not more criticism of current authors, but
more philosophy: more courage and sincerity in facing nature
directly, and in criticising books or institutions only with a view
to choosing among them whatever is most harmonious with the
life you want to lead. . . . I accordingly intend to devote such
years as may remain to me exclusively to philosophy; although I
hope the form in which it will be expressed will not lead you to
call it metaphysics."

Because Santayana believed that philosophy was something
else and something more than the quest after absolute truth,
because he was so plainly convinced that philosophy in the last

analysis is not a matter of proof but an activity of the disciplined imagination, there has always been some doubt that he should be considered a philosopher at all. Even William James wondered whether Santayana was quite serious about philosophy. But Santayana did not regard philosophy as a surrogate for science or a rational apology for faith. Its business was to be clear about the ends of life, to sort out and organize experience in the light of a conception of the good freely and deliberately adopted. And for all the cool urbanity and grace with which he expressed himself, Santayana was wholly committed to this conception of philosophy. George Santayana in fact is one of the few philosophers who set out to do openly and candidly what most philosophers have done covertly, halfheartedly, and without quite knowing what it was that they were doing. He set out to find what it was in nature and man that spoke most immediately to his heart of hearts.

The theme that moves through Santayana's philosophy is the theme of Aristotle: everything ideal has a natural basis and everything natural an ideal fulfillment. The theme was not new, and Santayana neither thought nor hoped that what he had to say about it was original. He was, he liked to say, "an ignorant man, almost a poet," and he hoped, rather, that he spoke out of the funded wisdom of the race. But when this theme was announced at the turn of the century in *The Life of Reason,* it broke upon a world still nagged by Victorian doubts, still worried that evolution, geology, and physics had proved that human ideals were random and meaningless, mere decorative foam on the wave of matter. *The Life of Reason* showed that man's ideals were as legitimate as ever, whatever his natural origins might be; more, in its judicious treatment of human religion, politics, science, and art, it showed that human aspirations were better grounded, more responsible, and more likely to be achieved when the natural conditions on which they depended were taken into account.

But it was not Santayana's abstract "message" that explains his magic. It was not even the limpid and epigrammatic prose in which he stated it. It was the mixture of irony and sympathy he brought to his great theme, the unrelenting standards combined with the unillusioned acceptance of men as they are; it was the epigrammatic wisdom and the literary imagination which evoked the inner experience of men living in the most disparate moral climates. Most of all, it was the expression of a frankly relativistic moral outlook that was nevertheless Dantesque in its stringent declaration of preferences, its comprehensiveness, and its consistency. Here was a man with the sobriety of Aristotle writing with the poetry and excitement of Plato on the only things which give anything else any meaning—human ideals.

For Santayana was interested in man and the world only as they suggested ideals on which the imagination could play. Perfection, he wrote in *The Sense of Beauty,* is "the ultimate justification of being," and he loved things only for the perfections they dimly foreshadowed. It was not the world as it is to which he was ultimately committed; it was not even the world as it might be. It was the ideal, in and for itself—"that vision of perfection," as he wrote to William James, "that we just catch, or for a moment embody in some work of art, or in some idealised reality: . . . the concomitant aspiration of life, always various, always beautiful, hardly ever expressible in its fulness."

But the man who wrote in *The Life of Reason* that ideals are not realizable "when they have no deep roots in the world" came to believe that no worthwhile ideals had very deep roots on the contemporary scene. The pressure of American life, its busyness, its puritanical sense that life was a battle to be won, its concentration on means and techniques, drove him away; World War I convinced him that the life of reason, the attempt to build a world in which ideals might be domesticated, was no longer really possible anywhere. A fanatic, in Santayana's famous definition, is a man who redoubles his efforts after he has forgotten his aims. The contemporary world, whether in its alarms and hysterias or in its mindless immersion in sheer activity, came to seem to Santayana a study in fanaticism.

So the romance or the tragedy of human reason and aspiration receded in the later Santayana, and the comedy of reason came into the foreground. The landscape was colder, and the man who described it wrote with neither desire nor hope. There is in him even a calculated irrelevance, a deliberate decision not to talk to what everyone else thinks is the point. Since his days as a Spanish-speaking boy in Boston, there had always been in Santayana the sense that he was an alien in the world; that sense came to dominate all his other impulses. He remained a thoroughgoing materialist as far as his beliefs about the executive order of nature were concerned; but he felt morally free to be a Platonist. The world was his host, and he was a spectator in it—uninvolved, detached, looking at things from the outside, with all the urgency and poison of existence taken out of them, and with only the timeless and finished patterns they suggest left in them. The later Santayana is the Proust among modern philosophers. In his earlier books it is the marvel of the emergence of human ideals out of the irrational flux of matter that excites him. In his later books it is the evanescence of human ideals, their meaninglessness except as images beheld by the mind, which occupies the center of his attention.

Ideals could not be built into the structure of the world. They could only be caught on the fly, contemplated for what they were, and let go.

Santayana read himself out of the world; and it is quite possible, as a consequence, that the world will not read him. His ethics had always had an ageless quality; they came to seem aged as well. His politics were not merely hostile to technology, commerce, and democracy; they became increasingly indifferent to most of the alternatives that are live options for modern men. There is much in his later work that is unfortunate—a display of questionable dialectic, an impressionism that verges on capriciousness, and something that can only be called attitudinizing. Everything becomes a myth, and nothing really tells us what is true or false. Religion, science, all human beliefs, are all equally metaphors, salutes to the unknowable, "so that the way is cleared for faith, in deciding which set of symbols one will trust." In the end, even Santayana's prejudices, always formidable, lost their consistency.

It is not just a change in fashions in thought, then, that explains why he holds an equivocal position today in our minds and memories. Quite apart from questions of technical philosophy, it is difficult to take firm hold of him as a man or as a commentator on the world. Santayana's sympathies for his fellows were imaginative and literary rather than direct. "If I take a practical part [in the world]," he said, "it is only by putting on a domino for the carnival. I am capable of that impulse, I can feel the fun and the intoxication of it; but the louder the rout the greater the frivolity, and the more complete the relief of stripping off the motley, washing away the paint, and returning to solitude, to silence, and to sincerity."

Few philosophers have had more capacity to penetrate inside points of view and ways of life foreign to their own—to re-create and represent them as living, palpable things. Was it precisely the emotional separateness of Santayana, his carefully guarded rootlessness, that gave him this capacity? If so, then the sense that he leaves of his separateness and distance from us—the sense that we cannot capture him or his ideas for any worldly cause or for any personal enthusiasm of our own—is the price, the very useful price, we pay for his genius. But there is another and more disagreeable price that we also pay. "In solitude it is possible to love mankind," wrote Santayana. "In the world, for one who knows the world, there can be nothing but secret or open war." His limitations, all his artificial, *fin-de-siècle* weariness and detachment, are caught in this judgment.

No one in this century has stated the Hellenic ideal of reason and civilization more contagiously or pertinently than Santayana did in *The Life of Reason*. Yet, while he scorned romantic egotism, he lived in Italy for many years, and there is no evidence in his autobiography or letters that he found Mussolini disagreeable or even comic. He lived through the Spanish-American War and the Nazi conquest of Europe—yet he has nothing bitter to say either about America's little venture into imperialism or Germany's great venture into madness. Instead, he expresses his scorn for William James, who was indignant at America's behavior, and he saves his contempt for his great *bête noire*, the philosophy of liberalism. Indeed, as he grew older, Santayana's detachment came to seem just mere crankiness, and his Olympian attitude really only a bad case of snobbishness. In an increasing number of his judgments words like "Anglo-Saxon," "American," "lower middle class," and "Jew" came to do heavy work indeed.

And yet what happens to Santayana's reputation will be a touchstone of the quality of our culture and of our growth in maturity and wisdom. "I don't know," he wrote William James about *The Life of Reason*, "if any one has felt in it something which, I am sure, is there: I mean the tears. . . . Much of the irritation which I may betray and which, I assure you, is much greater than I let it seem, comes of affection. It comes of exasperation at seeing the only things that are beautiful or worth having treated as if they were of no account." The tears are there in Santayana, early and late, for those who are willing to look for them. They explain why a man who wrote philosophy as a personal soliloquy spoke so contagiously and unforgettably to others. They explain why a man so ironical and disenchanted (in words he once used about Leopardi) "arrests us and rebukes us and delivers us."

Santayana's philosophy offers the portrait of a man who—in an age he thought hurried and mindless—retained a classic sense of the proportions and constancies of human life. Through Santayana's mind, the United States and the culture of this century are brought to the test of ancient ideals of human order and civilization. No moralist writing for an American audience has been at once so freethinking and idiosyncratic, so catholic, so profoundly orthodox and conservative. He cultivated his solitude because he prized his sincerity—his independence and his clarity about where he stood. In reading him, we can still discover the values of our own solitude and move toward the recovery of our sincerity.

IX

Four Illusions of Foreign Policy

AMERICAN MOODS ABOUT FOREIGN POLICY ARE NOTORIOUSLY variable. There are times, such as the Indian summer days that followed the Cuban crisis in 1962, when the American mood is high, and the feeling is in the air that the United States is in command of events. But there are other times when the mood is a mixture of resentment, surprise, and pessimism. We find ourselves asking—as we are asking about Viet Nam—how we got into the fix we are in and how we can get out of it. And we find ourselves wondering at such times whether there is any relation between our policies and the facts of the world—indeed, whether there is any relationship between the principles that, we believe or hope, govern our policies and the strategies, some amateurish, some Machiavellian, which we adopt to serve those principles.

Nor are these perplexities confined to Americans. At times the nation has astonished and pleased its friends, and given its adversaries pause, by the decisiveness of its reactions to events. At other times it has left both its friends and its opponents doubtful about the clarity and realism of its policies and the firmness of its national commitment.

Both at home and abroad, persisting through passing successes and failures, through shifts in mood and through changes in administration, there has, indeed, been a constant and nagging question: What is it about the American posture that makes people elsewhere less certain than we are about the clarity of our policies, the decency of our motives, or the strength of our national commitment? What is it that leads to the recurrent accusation here at home—no matter what administration may be in power—that American policy is essentially passive and defensive, doing little more than nibble at the fringes of events?

A large part of the answer, I venture to suggest, may lie in the fact that our policies are influenced by notions about the world that others do not share. Illusions which our conscious minds probably know to be untrue still dominate our first, spontaneous interpretation of events. They make our approach to the world defensive, negative, and anxious, and they take the breath of coherent and explicit ideas out of our policies. It is these illusions, I suspect, which are responsible, as much as anything else, for our habit of making mountains out of everyday dangers like Cuba while ignoring the mountainous, persisting emergency that produces such dangers.

The first of these illusions might be called the Illusion of Words. It shows itself in a tendency to treat certain words as things in themselves, and to deal with problems by throwing such words at them rather than by looking at the facts. Congress provided a good example only recently. The growing conflict between different centers of power within the so-called "Socialist camp" has been plainly visible for some time. Yet Congress, bemused by the phrase "international Communism," chose to act on the assumption that international Communism is tightly unified, and limited the discretion of the Executive in dealing with such countries as Poland and Yugoslavia. More respect for Communist professions of undying unity could not be shown by the most unthinking follower of the official party line. Such action suggests that the word "Communism" is the enemy, and not the complex phenomenon which the word actually designates.

Even when our war with words seems to produce nothing but verbal fireworks, the consequences are often serious. The influence of the Illusion of Words is shown in the subjects that serious men spend time discussing, and in the absurdities that sensible men have to bother to refute. For example, the Undersecretary of State not so long ago had to appear before a committee of Congress and explain, in the most solemn terms, that the cold war is not like a game, that you cannot add up points and keep a score, and that the slogan "no win" is a slogan without meaning. Similarly, a continuing issue in American politics has been the demand that more forceful action should be taken toward Cuba. But while the critics making this demand are certainly audible enough, they have not yet succeeded in spelling out the precise ways in which they would change the policies that have been followed.

Nor do we throw up this verbal smoke screen only where international affairs are concerned. The United States is the only nation in the Western alliance without a strong Socialist party, yet more fear of "socialism" is expressed every day in the United States than in any other country. The same tendency to see ghosts is displayed in the discussion of other domestic problems. From aid to education to the Supreme Court's decision on prayer in the schools, and from resistance to desegregation to a contest for county clerk, we can count on someone to announce that the fundamental issue is the Communist conspiracy.

This free way with words brings a quality of unreality to our public discussions. It leads some people to think we are hysterical, and it leads kinder observers to suspect that if we are not hysterical we are certainly rigid with logophobia. Happily, despite our apocalyptic political language, most American governments have been moderate and circumspect and have not normally moved precipitately or without calculating the consequences. Nevertheless, this is rather small consolation. For, even so, it still remains a mistake to think that words have no influence on our actions.

The tone of voice of radio and television reporters is regularly excited; newspapers too often inflate and inflame the events they report; commentators and workaday politicians, rushing to demonstrate that things are simple to men of clear moral vision like themselves, reduce the awful tragedies and surging hopes of this century to the terms of bad melodrama. Their immoderate words unnerve our friends, make it difficult for our opponents to know when to believe us, and deflect our attention and energies to false issues.

The hypnotic power that words have over us is a sign of other illusions. Among the most powerful of these is the Illusion of Stability. The American form of government has an unbroken history from the birth of the Republic. With one very large exception—the problem of slavery and of relations between Negroes and whites—our constitutional processes have served as the framework within which Americans have successfully solved most of their problems and regulated the vigorous struggles between individuals and groups in our society. Against this background of experience, it is natural that we should take orderly political processes for granted, and that we should believe in the efficacy of democratic methods when employed in good faith.

But this experience has also created a quasi-instinctive assumption that stability is the normal order of human affairs. At worst, this leads to the view that violent upheavals are the work of men who are too ignorant, too impatient, or too ruthless to work for their goals in a legal way. At best, it leads to a preoccupation with the immediate causes of instability and to neglect of the long-range problems involved in achieving a degree of stability that is in fact quite unusual. For it is a mistake to imagine that once tyrants are removed, or the economic conditions in a troubled area are improved, the subsequent course of events will automatically bring peace and democracy.

Probably, we really know better. The Civil War and our present difficulties with desegregation suggest the limitations of this instinctive attitude. But if we do know better we know it only fitfully and regretfully. Our initial reaction to the whirling world in which we live is still one of surprise, and our public debate betrays bewilderment, nostalgia, and a wistful hope for some quick and easy way to make things hold still again.

Another closely connected illusion is the Illusion of a Classless Society. In America, the boundaries between social classes have always been loosely drawn. To be sure, we have sharp differences in the distribution of wealth and income; there are barriers against marriage and free communication between members of different groups, and inherited advantages and disadvantages certainly affect the chances in life of different individuals. Still, whether correctly or not, Americans, for the most part, do not regard any of these differences as insurmountable. They assume that able and ambitious individuals can generally find their proper levels in society by using natural talents and energies. And certainly there are in the United States fewer outward signs of social deference than are present in most other societies.

All this leads us to misunderstand or ignore one of the most important aspects of most revolutionary movements. We can understand a political revolution, which is an attempt to install one form of government in place of another. With somewhat greater difficulty we have come to understand that revolutions may also have economic aspects, and that they are brought about by people who want a better standard of living and changes in the distribution of wealth and opportunity. But we do not as yet quite perceive or conceive of the phenomenon of *social* revolution.

In a social revolution, those who have been on the outside looking in, those who have been treated as second-class and second-rate, are struggling to get some of their own back. They do not want simply a change in the form of government or a better standard of living. They want a change in the status of the group to which they belong. They want to move in places where they could not move before, to walk along fashionable streets, perhaps even to break a few fashionable windows. They want to put their own people in—or those they think are their own people—and drive the others out.

It is not impossible to carry out such a revolution peacefully, but it is difficult. Efforts by the United States to help the developing countries are unlikely to succeed, therefore, unless this bitter, social aspect of revolutionary movements is taken into account. Our frequent failure to do so is another reason why

American political thinking so often seems to others to be above the battle and not quite to the point.

Finally, there is a special and curious illusion which, I believe, even captures some of the shrewdest and most energetic of our policy makers. I would call it the Illusion of the Practical. It consists in the tacit assumption that a series of resolute and ingenious tactical operations is all that there is to a foreign policy—that the capacity to meet emergencies and to deal with them successfully is the be-all and end-all.

Ingenuity, a capacity to improvise, a distrust of established doctrines, and an ability to marshal resources and act decisively in moments of crisis have no doubt had much to do with the conquest of our continent and the development of the American economic and political system. Perhaps this is the reason why we find it hard to develop a firm policy on any particular issue until an emergency arises. Indeed, there are those who believe that this preserves us against the abstract plans, programs, and theories that have seduced so many other societies. The actual issues that have to be met when emergencies arise, these antitheoretical theorists point out, are always more complex, more prickly with unexpected contingencies, than any plan or policy can foresee. Only a program forged in the furnace of actual events, they maintain, and not a program formulated for hypothetical circumstances, can deal with such emergencies.

This is true enough, but a number of other things are true as well. The notion that policy is made in emergencies means that policy will only be focused on emergencies. This may have made sense when the world was a friendlier place and we could expect that the normal flow of events between emergencies would be favorable to us, but a somewhat less optimistic view seems called for today. A program like the Alliance for Progress, for example, requires more than resources, dedication, and diplomatic skill. It requires some guiding ideas about the processes of modernization and the evolution of democracy, so that conscious and studied decisions about social priorities can be made. Ideas are not, of course, magical formulas that will resolve all problems or make events lie down and behave as they are told. But ideas are present, nevertheless, even in the policies of men who distrust ideas, and long-range decisions about social priorities are often made quite unconsciously by men who imagine that they are dealing only with an immediate emergency. One of the simplest reasons for having a carefully wrought policy is to make it plain to such men that they have such ideas and are making such decisions. The Illusion of the Practical tends to hide this from them. And it deprives American policy of the sense of meaning and purpose, and of the excitement, it might otherwise have.

There is always a kind of popular undertow against which the formulation of foreign policy in America has to play—a desire for action, an indisposition to sit still. This has its manifest dangers. Properly disciplined and directed, however, it also provides one of the elements that can make American policy successful. If an American government could make its program for the more distant future clear and affirmative enough, and if it could pursue that program vividly in the here and now, the American desire for action might be marshaled for the long pull and not just for fitful explosions of energy at moments of crisis.

Such a program would probably not cost more in money nor would it be more dangerous than the quasipolicies we follow now. It would require, however, a willingness and capacity to be candid about fundamentals, to use words with respect for their meaning, and to imagine the condition, hates, and hopes of people whose experience has not been like our own. Most difficult of all, it would require an encounter with ourselves—a critical awareness of our own habits of mind, and an effort to break free from the protective illusions that damage our power to act in the world as it exists.

X

———— ⚜ ————

Unphilosophical Pragmatism

THE TIME IS OVERDUE TO ASK QUESTIONS ABOUT THE EXCES-
sive use of one of the sacred words in the contemporary American vocabulary. The word is "pragmatism." Businessmen, dip-
lomats, policemen, and leaders of mass protest movements all
boast of their pragmatism. Eminent clergymen recall us
strongly to the everlasting truths of God, and then hasten to add
that these truths must of course be interpreted pragmatically.
And if a man is not quite sure where he is going or what he is
trying to do, he can always say that he is proceeding pragmatically. This is even better than an explanation of his actions.
It makes it seem naïve to ask for an explanation.

Are we Americans as pragmatic as we seem to think we are?
Should we congratulate ourselves for being pragmatic? And
what does "pragmatism" mean anyway? These questions go to
the heart of American culture and the American moral style.
And the answers we give to them—the answers implicit in our
actions as well as the answers we put into words—have a bearing
on our domestic economy, foreign policy, cities, schools, and
political and intellectual life.

In the sense in which most people probably use the term,
"pragmatism," at first blush, simply seems to mean "being prac-

tical." To be pragmatic is to take a down-to-earth view of things. It is to recognize that, in this vale of tears and ineptitude, you cannot aim at perfection but must be content with anything that will work. You must avoid big theories and rigid principles, you must face your problems one at a time, and you must be ready to improvise because you certainly will have to.

The organizers of a new business enterprise, for example, may have a very clear idea of what they would like the enterprise to be in five years, and of what needs to be done to get it there. But they find, after they start to work, that not all these things can be done. They also find that a good many other things are happening, some good and some bad, which were not forecast in their original plans. So they decide to proceed "pragmatically," taking up their problems as they come, making the best of their opportunities, and hoping that, in five years, if they are not where they originally hoped they would be, they will be someplace else equally good. And such a pragmatic approach can be adopted just as well by a technical-aid mission to a foreign country or by a doctor treating a chronically ill patient.

And yet, when such an approach is adopted and advertised as "pragmatic," it cannot be described simply as an everyday "practical" approach. For it is an *approach,* an expression of a point of view, a more or less consistent and deliberate way of doing things. To be "pragmatic" is to be much more than simply "practical." It is to be "practical"—whatever that means —as a matter of principle. When a man says that he is being pragmatic, he means to say that he is doing something more than just living from day to day. There is in his actions, he seems to be implying, a conscious program, a special kind of wisdom.

Indeed, the word "practical" really solves few problems when it is offered as a synonym for "pragmatic." For what we mean by "practical" depends on the standards we employ to define efficiency or success, and these are notoriously divergent. Theoretical Marxists, philosophical anarchists, and Christian martyrs have not chosen their positions because they have thought them impractical. On the contrary, these opponents of pragmatism have believed that only their positions are really likely to work, and that it is pragmatism which is unworkable.

What, then, *is* pragmatism? In the most common sense of the term, it is an attitude toward life. And like other attitudes toward life, it is soaked in unexamined philosophical commitments—in beliefs about the nature of the world, in moral principles and prejudices, in conceptions about the uses of life and the afterlife. Particularly in the case of pragmatism, these philosophical commitments are usually unacknowledged and even unconscious, but this does not make them any less important. Pragmatism does not represent simply an interest in being practical; it represents a particular view of what it means to be practical. Pragmatism does not simply propose a strategy for getting ahead in any kind of world; it assumes that the world has a certain normal shape, so that only certain ways of getting ahead are likely to work.

Let us try to describe this attitude, then, bearing in mind that we are describing not philosophical pragmatism, which is a studied, argued, and self-conscious approach to the world, but popular pragmatism, a more everyday, rough-and-ready affair. (Whether philosophical pragmatism and popular pragmatism are related is something we must ask; but for the moment let us suspend judgment.) The first characteristic of pragmatism as an attitude toward life, I would say, is its distrust of doctrines and creeds, its suspicion of words and argumentation. The pragmatist prefers action to talk, he is restless for results, and he normally counts "results" in terms of some physical or visible difference that has been made in the world. He is not necessarily disrespectful of such things as religion or philosophy, but neither is he overawed by any man's religion or philosophy. He wants to see the difference they make in the way a man lives.

For the pragmatist implicitly assumes that in the arenas where the real business of the world gets done life is too rough and ready for fine-spun distinctions, and too fluid and diversified to fit any theories. He treasures flexibility, so that he can get along in these arenas. And what he fears is the beguiling formula that can prevent him from using his horse sense, the fixed principle that will not let him change his plans in midpassage, the learned foolishness of the great theories and philosophies which can keep him from looking facts in the face. The pragmatic mind rejects an elaborate social theory like Marxism not because it has another theory which it thinks is a better one but because all theories seem to it a little ingenuous —indeed, a little bizarre—in this tricky world.

Closely connected to this distrust of general ideas is the pragmatic attitude toward serious reflection on the goals and ends of life. Generally speaking, a pragmatist says nothing about the goals of life. On the contrary, he seems to suspect that such talk is merely a way of avoiding the real business of life, which is to get down to work. He tends to believe—if "belief" is the right word for anything so instinctive—that if the physical side of life is buttoned up neatly, if the safety, convenience, and comfort of life are enhanced, most of the so-called spiritual problems will lose their urgency. So he is impatient with people who waste their time and the limited resources of mankind by sitting around asking questions that can never be answered.

Nor is there only crudity of mind in this attitude. The pragmatist is suspicious of discussion of the ends of life, as often as not, because experience has taught him that such discussion usually generates heat but no light, and creates hostilities that prevent men from getting together to deal with problems they might otherwise be able to solve. Moreover, he assumes that you are merely whistling in the dark when you talk about all your high purposes but never get down to the question of how to reach them. Indeed, he is convinced that what men accomplish generally depends more on the methods they use than on the purposes they profess.

Finally, the pragmatist has a shrewd insight into the way in which creative activity takes place. The pragmatist is likely to be a man who has discovered what many active doers, including doers in the arts, sciences, and philosophy, have discovered—that one cannot know what one is trying to do until one has done it, that one only finds one's purposes and ends in the process of acting. And the pragmatist rather enjoys this human predicament. He has more confidence in human purposes that have been forged in action than in those laid down as part of a prearranged plan.

Equally to the point, although he recognizes the risks in a policy of leaping and then looking, this is likely to add to the zest the pragmatist feels for the enterprise. For he assumes, in the end, that the world takes managing, but that it can be managed—that it exists as a theater for the exercise of his ingenuity and courage, and that if he has a sufficient supply of these commodities, there isn't much that the world will not let him do. It is an open world, a world in which men, if they are strong-willed enough, can will into existence a large part of whatever it is that they desire.

But what is it that the pragmatist thinks that men desire, or ought to desire? We come to the ultimate value judgment buried in the pragmatic *Weltanschauung,* the basic reason why it pays so little attention to questions of ends and purposes. The great purpose, for the spontaneous pragmatist, is nothing else but the exercise of human ingenuity and resolution, nothing else but the solving of problems whatever they may be. Not rest but motion, not yesterday's victory but the prospect of tomorrow's, not where you are going but the excitement and pleasure and the demonstration of power that accompany getting there— these are what give life its savor to the pragmatist.

If there is any conception of progress, of cumulative improvement, in this glorification of motion, it is the idea of improvement in Method and Technique, in knowledge and in power. And if there is any controlling faith behind the notion that the advance of human ingenuity means an advance in human decency and happiness, it is the faith that most of those who play the pragmatic game will be gregarious, sportsmanlike fellows who love the game for its own sake and want to keep it going. If pragmatism as an everyday attitude is to prevail and to succeed, there has to be, therefore, a reservoir of mutual trust and good will in society, and some fairly firm and restraining norms of behavior. And this, of course, is precisely what most everyday advocates of everyday pragmatism have assumed to be the case. The essential stability and decency of society, and the existence of a basic moral consensus, have been the unspoken premises on which popular pragmatism has rested. For only under such conditions can the concentration on Method and the love of Technique not collapse into pure Machiavellianism.

Are Americans, then, pragmatic? Do most of us normally act on the set of assumptions and principles that have just been described? We must be careful how we answer this question.

One common way to answer it, for example, particularly abroad, is to point to the fact that a technical philosophy known as "pragmatism" has been developed here and that it is mainly an American creation. This is true. The very word "pragmatism," in fact, was invented about eighty years ago by the philosopher Charles Peirce, the author of most of philosophical pragmatism's important ideas.

But to say, as so many foreign observers do, that this philosophy is our national creed is to pay us an undeserved compliment. Philosophical pragmatism has certain resemblances to the common, garden-variety kind of unphilosophical pragmatism we have been discussing. But in the most important respect it is the very reverse of what is commonly meant by pragmatism. Its most important insight has to do with the key importance of *ideas* as regulators and directors of human experience. It is, in fact, a restatement of the old philosophical dream that men might be guided in their lives by ideas and principles they have deliberately examined and chosen. Whatever may be said against this philosophy, it does not suffer from lack of sufficient respect for ideas. If it errs, it is in the unrealistic hopes it entertains concerning the role that philosophy and reasonable ideas might play in the governance of human affairs. And if Americans are pragmatic in the ordinary meaning of the term, it follows that at least in certain respects they will not feel any special friendliness for philosophical pragmatism.

But *are* Americans pragmatic? The answer, it seems to me, is Yes and No. Probably we are more action oriented than a good many other people, more content to move along case by case, and readier to place our trust simply in the expansion of human ingenuity and power without worrying about the purposes to which this ingenuity and power might be put. This spontaneous pragmatism was more characteristic of us a generation ago, perhaps, than it is today, but even today our economy is characterized by a passion for technology, our social science by a faith in methodology, and our approach to the world, as illustrated by our first ventures in foreign aid, by an apparent conviction that if men have the requisite know-how, and can solve their material problems, most of their other problems will fall into place. Religions in America too have emphasized an ethic rather than a creed, a feeling of commitment rather than a theology. Nowhere else has the tendency been so strong to compress Christianity into a social gospel or to identify it so largely with the ideals of secular democracy.

Yet this is far from the whole story. Side by side with our pragmatic suspicion of absolutes, there have been chiliastic religions in America warning of the devil and preaching the millennium. Our politics too has a recurrent millennial strain in it. Although most American politicians show a capacity to deal and compromise, and a shrewd refusal to believe that the world is about to come to an end, our public debate remains cramped by apocalyptic language and rigid creeds, and is unduly deferential to ideological bogeymen and simplistic theories of history. And whenever we come to issues which people regard as matters of ultimate principle—the integration of Negroes into American life is the prime example—the inaccuracy of the description of Americans as "pragmatic" becomes painfully evident.

Even more important, it is when we turn to such questions, it seems to me, that the limitations of pragmatism become clear. The assumptions of pragmatism, as we have remarked, are justified only under rather special conditions—only when the moral consensus in society is deep and wide and only when the basic institutions of a society appear to be reasonably stable.

The unspoken conviction that lies behind the reliance on pragmatism as a method of social action is that most problems can be licked if only good fellows get together and use the brains God gave them. It is a conviction, it must be said, that is often justified pragmatically when it is acted upon. It tends to *make* good fellows. For when men act on it, they often find that it is easier than they had supposed to put aside their rigid principles and to work out their difficulties with others cooperatively.

But this assumption does not work invariably. It does not work when decisions of principle are involved that cannot be postponed or finessed. For sometimes decisions of principle can be postponed or finessed; but not always. In the case of racial segregation, for example, the issue at stake is not, in fact, this or that limited reform. It is a matter of principle—the recognition of the Negro's equal status with all other citizens and his full membership in American society. Better schools or housing, or more job opportunities do not settle this matter of principle; and even more important, such pragmatic approaches are not likely to be effective unless the matter of principle has been settled. Only in such a context can the pragmatic method of mutual concession take over. Ultimately this is why the passage of legislation like the civil rights law is important. Such legislation has some direct practical significance, but its most important use is symbolic. It registers the fact that the representatives of the nation, duly assembled, have decided an issue of principle. Within the framework of such a decision, it is then possible to speak of conciliation and compromise.

In general, the pragmatic distrust of abstract creeds is not a workable attitude at times when social change is rapid and radical. At such times people cannot be expected automatically to accommodate themselves to change, and bit by bit to learn the new ways of thinking and feeling that will fit them to their new environment. They are likely to need some sense of where they are going and why they are undergoing the experiences that they are. They need to be able to interpret and understand what is happening to them. Pragmatism, *tout court,* does not answer this need. Worse still, in its apparent indifference to the problem, it tacitly implies that jobs, schools, or a new government bureau are quite adequate substitutes for a clear sense of direction and an understanding of the meaning of events. This weakness in pragmatism becomes particularly conspicuous when the attitude is transported overseas and Americans make the effort to work together with, and to understand and be understood by, the members of developing nations.

Indeed, there is in pragmatism a special moral orientation which we cannot expect that everyone will share. The pragmatic mind tends to think that the merit of an idea is the power it gives in action, that the reason for a comment on life is to improve life. But it is just as easy to take the reverse position, and to think that the reason for life is the chance to comment on it. In many parts of the world civilized men, and this includes a great many who are poor, simply do not find their greatest delight in successful negotiation or busy practical action. They find more importance, and take more immediate pleasure, in the significant gesture that releases an emotion, in the story that illuminates a situation, in the action that dramatizes an issue or makes a principle indelibly plain. The values they seek—the "results" they expect—in their daily lives and in the public arena are primarily contemplative and theatrical, not practical or muscular. They prefer a sense of understanding, and perhaps a feeling of amusement, to the satisfactions of a job well done.

The virtues are not all on their side. One of the uses of ideas is that they are generally neater, cleaner, and more orderly than the complex world of action. This is why they give pleasure, and why many men prefer an approach to life and to politics that allows them to enjoy their ideas untroubled by petty questions of ways, means, and procedures. But it is also easy to see why this kind of politics—the politics of rhetoric, of the café and the drawing room and the students' quarters, the politics which is a principal amusement of many nations in the world—should not appeal to a normal, sober, sensible, impatient pragmatist. On the contrary, it is likely to leave him surprised and indignant, unpragmatic as such emotions may be.

For the faith of pragmatism is that men can make better lives for themselves if only they forswear doctrinaire arguments and turn to practical questions on which they can cooperate. And it is intellectualistic self-hypnosis to sneer at this faith as vulgar, materialistic, or antihumanistic. It is a noble faith. Those who have acted on it have put out many fires while the doctrinaire have fiddled with their theories. Many of the greatest achievements of American history are undoubtedly due to this pragmatism, and the international scene would be much worse today if this pragmatism did not play a part in our behavior.

And yet, when American pragmatism seems to be nothing but unrelieved busyness, nothing but smiling good will and an inability to sit still, it can repel many who would otherwise be sympathetic to it. Pragmatism ignores the fact that many people want more from politics and social change than the improvement of their physical well-being. They want a sense of coherent and overarching purpose; they want meaning. Pragmatism works, as it has in the United States, only when that question of meaning is largely settled, only when the general direction of events seems clear and desirable. That is why a "pragmatic approach," and nothing more, in areas like Latin America is pragmatically self-defeating.

It is also, I am inclined to think, why we cannot rely on the pragmatic method in the United States to the extent that we have in the past. Rapid and intense social changes have left a great many Americans with acute feelings of disorientation. Much of our politics is more obviously an effort to supply the catchwords that will relieve these feelings of disorientation than it is to debate the practical issues confronting the nation. That is why the abstractions and ideologies, just when we think that we have finally got them tamed, break in on our pleasant, pragmatic proceedings again and again, and always a little to our surprise.

For the desire for meaning, the acute aversion to a sense of disorientation, is a factor of the greatest importance in politics. And it cannot be conjured away simply by the pragmatic magic of good will and good works. The great pragmatic fallacy is to assume that people want action and not also a scheme of action, that they merely want to get where they are going and have no interest in a general map of the territory through which they are traveling. But this is not true. It is no longer true even of many quite pragmatic Americans. The pace of change has become too rapid; it is not emotionally assimilable unless the mind can detect a larger pattern in events. For all its cheerful, healthy, down-to-earth attractions, pragmatism will have to be supplemented by philosophy.

XI

John Dewey's Legacy

Even during his lifetime John Dewey suffered the unfortunate fate that the gods seem to reserve for those who become too influential in philosophy. He disappeared as an individual and became a symbol. Plato, it will be remembered,
fought in his letters to preserve the image of his poor singular
self, and insisted that what he had taught could not be con-
densed into a doctrine. Even Karl Marx felt the need to remind
his friends wistfully that, after all, he himself was not a Marxist.
And it is difficult now to remember that John Dewey was a
man, not an institution, a philosopher and not a social movement.

For more than two generations the mention of this unassum-
ing man's name has been less an invitation to the discussion of
his philosophy than a signal for the start of large debates about
the ailments of the modern world. To be for Dewey has been to
be for progress, reason, and enlightenment. To be against him
has been to be on the side of God, the ancient values of our
civilization, and the triumph of spirit over matter. To himself
Dewey must have seemed to be what any philosopher who is not
self-deceived must seem to himself to be—an individual, work-

ing ultimately in solitude, plagued by doubts, impatient with his deficiencies, and taking a chance on such ideas as he might happen to have. But to his admirers Dewey was and is a representation of all that is most hopeful in American civilization. And to his detractors he was and remains a paradigm of some of the worst ills of our society.

Indeed, even those for whom Dewey's name is not a battle cry find it difficult to approach his work with detachment. For whatever Dewey's influence may really have been, his ideas are in the air and his name has echoes. He stood astride an era in American thought with which we are still busy making our peace. To read Dewey's works is to be forced to ask what we ourselves, facing our own problems, really think about progressive education, the Welfare State, the moral implications of science, the meaning of liberalism, or almost any one of the other contemporary issues around which intellectual controversies rage. Even when we turn to aspects of the present scene with which Dewey cannot be associated—the vogue of Zen Buddhism or existentialist theology at one extreme and the influence of linguistic philosophy on the other—Dewey's image comes to mind, teasing us to decide whether we have fallen from grace or have finally begun to recover our senses. For Dewey stands there as a palpable presence, a possible alternative. To know where we stand toward Dewey's ideas is to find out, at least in part, where we stand with ourselves.

It may be good to be reminded, therefore, that he was born more than a hundred years ago. For he lived so long and vigorously, he remains so inextricably associated in the public mind with what is "new" and "progressive," and he is still so substantial a figure among us, that it is easy to forget that he grew up in a world very different from our own. Indeed, the problems that gave Dewey's thought the shape it retained throughout his life were different in fundamental ways from the problems we face.

Dewey was born before Lincoln was President. He was fifty-five years old when the long peace of the nineteenth century collapsed into permanent war, revolution, and tension. When he was a graduate student at Johns Hopkins, the most speculative of philosophies, idealism, dominated the university scene, and not the most antispeculative of philosophies, logical empiricism. The great idea that had to be absorbed into Western thinking was the theory of evolution. Socialism was a mere ideal, Communism in Russia unthinkable, Fascism unimagined. And Freud was unheard of, Kierkegaard forgotten, and the Orient a reality only to exotics.

In the law and social thinking Dewey was faced by the principles of Social Darwinism and the doctrine of "natural rights" applied to the behavior of impersonal corporations. In economics he saw unbridled competition, on one side, and insecurity and indignity for masses of men, on the other. In politics he had to worry about a state that did too little, not a state that did too much. In the schools there was political patronage, antiquarianism, and a discipline so senseless that children might even be prohibited from turning their heads in class. And in American intellectual life generally Dewey had to wrestle not so much with the slick vulgarity that troubles us today but with prudishness, gentility, and conceptions of culture and the good life to which only a few in a democratic and industrial age could hope to aspire.

What does a man who grew up in such a world, and whose basic ideas were shaped as answers to such problems, have to say to us? The question is all the more pertinent because Dewey was so honestly and eagerly a creature of his time. And it becomes more insistent when we examine the curious equipment that Dewey brought to his philosophical tasks.

To begin with, he wrote badly—almost, indeed, as though it were a matter of principle. Most of his books were unorganized and repetitious, many of his arguments imprecise and incomplete. At times his sentences have vigor and bite. At other times we enter a sentence of Dewey's and find ourselves in a trackless thicket, from which we emerge at the other end scratched, shaken, and relieved. In Dewey's hands even individual words play tricks on us, snarling when we expect them to purr, evaporating when we expect them to stand for something solid. Dewey did not invent his own system of notation, but he did not write in ordinary English either. With some help from his long apprenticeship in German idealism, he made ordinary English over into an artificial tongue.

To be sure, there was a purpose behind this semantic mayhem. Dewey had a sense of the nuances of terms and a shrewd Yankee judgment about their ambiguities. He saw, or thought he saw, that many words we habitually use—including words like "experience," "reality," "true," and "good," which are fundamental in building our conception of the world and our place in it—have quite the wrong meanings attached to them as a result of their historical careers. He wanted to squeeze the wrong meanings out of these words and attach new and better meanings to them. So he used the words not as they are ordinarily used but as he thought they ought to be used, and he frequently gave old terms new depth and power in the process.

Unfortunately, however, he did not always remember that his readers needed to be warned about what he was doing. And he frequently replaced an old ambiguity simply with a new and more troublesome ambiguity. Surely, for example, it is confusing to remark, as Dewey once did, that his book *Experience and Nature* might just as easily have been called *Culture and Nature*, and that the title would not have changed its meaning with this change in its terms. Whatever the reasons may have been, Dewey wrote tortuously, inexactly, carelessly.

Nor is it only Dewey's prose that we must take into account in considering his deficiencies. It must also be said, I think, that Dewey regularly ignored important ideas and issues that were clearly relevant to the themes he chose to discuss. He wrote about logic, but he was largely indifferent to symbolic logic and the revolutionary work of Bertrand Russell and Alfred North Whitehead. He devoted much of his time to questions about the growth of personality and the education of children. But even though he continued to pay attention to these questions after 1920, he did less than disagree with Freud: he virtually ignored his existence.

Perhaps most disconcerting of all, Dewey repeatedly claimed that his ideas were supported by the logic of science and pleaded continually for the use of scientific method in all fields. But the examples of scientific thinking that Dewey offered and analyzed were only rarely examples of scientific thought at its theoretical or system-building levels. They were much more often examples taken from practical life—a doctor diagnosing a disease, an engineer planning a bridge. Compared with Russell, Whitehead, Morris Cohen, or even Josiah Royce—to mention only a few of his distinguished contemporaries in philosophy—Dewey's knowledge of the sciences, and particularly of mathematics and the physical sciences, was secondhand.

Dewey had, to be sure, an original and powerful insight into certain issues. He is clearly one of those most responsible for helping us to recognize the constructive and creative aspects of scientific thought and the difference that scientific habits of mind make in any culture that accepts them. But in the history of the interpretation of science there are men like Francis Bacon or Voltaire, who look at science from the outside, seize on some one of its features, and then go on to explain to the non-scientist the general difference that science can make in human attitudes or in standards of right reason. There are, on the other hand, men like Descartes or Immanuel Kant, who understand science from the inside, and who deal, so to speak, with some of its professional problems of logic and method as well as with its general relation to other styles of life and thought. Dewey falls somewhere between these two groups. He was neither so clear and dramatic nor quite so superficial as Bacon or Voltaire. But he did not have the precise grasp of details or the informed authority of Kant or of other philosophers in the American tradition, like Charles Peirce.

In fact, there is rather generally a curious remoteness about Dewey, a habit of talking around a subject without coming to close grips with it. He showed this trait even when he dealt with subjects about which he knew a good deal. Much of his philosophic writing, for example, consists of criticisms of the great historical traditions in philosophy. There are few historians of philosophy at work today, however, who would not regard the picture that Dewey drew of his philosophic ancestors as slanted and inaccurate. Again, although Dewey's central interest was in social affairs, one cannot find anywhere in his work a direct, systematic examination of major social philosophies—for example, competitive capitalism, socialism, anarchism, syndicalism, guild socialism—that were competing for men's allegiance in his day.

In short, although Dewey argued that philosophy must be a guide to the solution of concrete, practical problems, he repeatedly left his readers guessing what he himself thought about such issues. He was a man of rugged courage who was not afraid to take sides in public controversies. But in his writing he regularly stopped at just the point where we are anxious to see, if only in outline, the kind of practical, positive program he thought his ideas implied. He was a social reformer whose position toward socialism in America, even in the thirties, was unclear. He was a writer on morals who never discussed questions of sexual morality. He was an innovator in education whose views about progressive education are still a legitimate subject for debate. He was modest and had good sense, and this may explain why he was unwilling to pontificate in areas where no man, and least of all a philosopher, can be sure of himself. But it cannot explain the difficulty there is in determining where Dewey stood, simply as one man among other men, on many of the issues that he himself raised for discussion.

What, then, remains? Why did Dewey make the stir that he did? What did he leave that was important, and that we can choose to forget only at a great loss to ourselves?

The answer can be found, I think, only if we are prepared to look at Dewey from a point of view that is not habitual in philosophical circles today. He did not have some of the qualities that a professional philosopher ought to have. He was not an elegant thinker and not always a disciplined one. But he had a quality which can make the difference between a merely skillful philosopher and a first-rate original mind. In his own cheerful, unaggressive way he was a visionary.

It is not easy to think of this quiet, patient man in this way.

He was easygoing, unimpassioned, and temperate. He did not go in for flights of fancy or bursts of indignation, or indulge in the consolations of paradox and irony like those other visionaries of his generation, Shaw and Russell. He simply kept going, year after year, sticking to his guns, insistent, indefatigable, and always returning—the sure mark of a visionary—to the same basic theme.

And it was a distinctive theme, which the comparison with Shaw and Russell highlights. Shaw was fundamentally disturbed, as he once remarked, by stupidity; it was the direction of life by a consistent view of things that excited him. In Russell's work there are the twin visions of certainty in intellectual matters and justice in the arrangement of human affairs. But while Dewey did not like stupidity and injustice, what basically disturbed him was the decline of any human being's life into a state of passivity. It seemed to him to be the denial of the human birthright.

There is a sentence in Karl Marx's *Kapital* which, with appropriate alterations, suggests what Dewey thought the basic human problem of his day was. Under capitalism, Marx wrote, the advance of technology and the accumulation of capital, far from helping the worker, "mutilate the laborer into a fragment of a man, degrade him to the level of appendage to a machine, destroy every remnant of charm in his work and turn it into hated toil." Dewey could not speak with the scorn and bitterness of a Hebrew prophet. Moreover, he thought too steadily in terms of the individual's day-to-day experience to believe that an abstract change in the law of property would be enough to change a man's relation to his work. He would have asked whether factories were still organized in an authoritarian manner or whether the economic revolution had been imposed without the consent of those affected. And he would have looked at other areas where human behavior is governed and human personality is shaped or misshaped—for example, at philosophies that suggest that the answer to men's problems can be found simply by consulting fixed principles, or at educational systems that make submissiveness the child's central experience in the classroom.

But Dewey would have agreed that it was the "mutilation" of the individual, the imposition upon him of an external, mechanical routine, which was the basic moral problem of industrial society. He would have thought, indeed, that it had been the moral problem of all major forms of social organization that had ever existed. And he would have felt an immediate sympathy, it may be suspected, with the direct language, the immediate and aesthetic language, that Marx employed in this passage. For the program of reconstruction in philosophy, morals, and society which Dewey proposed can be understood only if we see that Dewey took the daily experience of individuals more seriously than he took anything else, and that he ultimately evaluated everything as an instrument for the enrichment of such experience.

This is the heart of Dewey's philosophy, I suggest, and the ultimate meaning that is to be attached to calling him a "pragmatist" or "instrumentalist." What Dewey wanted to see diffused throughout human life, and what he thought that democracy, science, and technology could diffuse, were qualities that we find best exemplified in the arts—spontaneity, self-discipline, the involvement of the personality, and the marriage of individuality and order, the delightful and the meaningful. His enemies were routine, drill, external dictation, and the readymade in ideas; and the targets he attacked were social arrangements, educational methods, or philosophical systems that seemed to promote such qualities.

Oddly enough, this philosopher who wrote so badly, whose thinking seems so homely and prosaic, and who is remembered for his glorification of science, had essentially a poet's vision of the possibilities of human life. He wished to see men's environments so ordered that the life of art was possible for all. His ideal was a world in which individuals lived with a sense of active purpose, exerting their individual powers, putting their mark on their environments, sharing their experiences, and making their own contribution to the common enterprises of humanity. He did not seem to think that this was a utopian ideal—or perhaps he did not care if it was. For he was convinced that it could be more closely approximated in the modern world than it had ever been before, and it was the only ideal which could give our power and wealth some meaning beyond themselves.

"Democracy," Dewey once wrote, and he said the same thing in one way or another again and again, "is belief in the ability of human experience to generate the aims and methods by which further experience will grow in ordered richness." It is an odd definition, and a dark one. But it becomes clearer when we put it alongside a remark he made in his book on aesthetics, *Art as Experience*. "Ultimately," Dewey wrote, "there are but two philosophies. One of them accepts life and experience in all its uncertainty, mystery, doubt and half-knowledge and turns that experience upon itself to deepen and intensify its own qualities—to imagination and art. This is the philosophy of Shakespeare and Keats."

It is a long way from the poetry of Shakespeare and Keats to a philosophy of democracy, but Dewey had a way of bringing distant things together. And the bridge by which he made such transitions was his theory of human experience—his conception of human life in its ideal form. He rejected any philosophy that seemed to cut human life or society to a prearranged form. He preferred philosophies that liberated men from leading strings and allowed them to take control of their own lives. And so he framed his moral philosophy, his educational theory, and his conception of democracy not primarily in terms of abstract ideals or institutional arrangements, but in terms of the diffusion throughout a society of this distinctive sort of personal experience.

This is the vision that stands behind the freshness and power of John Dewey's insights. With this vision he turned logic, the history of philosophy, and even that most abstruse and apparently artificial of philosophical subjects—the theory of knowledge—into subjects with moral and cultural significance. He connected theory not only to practice but to a coherent image of what human life might be. And he made philosophy what it has always been when it has been most vigorous—a commentary on things outside itself and a challenge to men to make up their minds about the terms on which they are willing to conduct their business in this world. Underneath the difficulties of his language and the technicalities of his arguments Dewey's vision, it seems to me, is the source of the excitement and the sense of importance that his work communicated, and still communicates, to others.

Despite the looseness and occasional tedium of John Dewey's books, they have, then, an inner dynamism. There is a coherent theory of experience that propels them. This theory is best formulated in *Art as Experience,* the most revealing of Dewey's books, I think, and the one to which too little attention is paid.

But it also controls Dewey's thinking in his books on education, morals, democracy, and science. What was this theory? To what notions about human culture did it lead Dewey? How did it affect his philosophy of education and of science? These are the questions to which we must turn.

There are for Dewey two extremes between which our experience moves. At one extreme we live by habits, which include, of course, habits of mind and feeling as well as habits of motor behavior. Without habits our lives would be unendurable: every action that was not instinctive would call for a decision. And so long as we do not meet new situations in which our habits come a cropper, our lives move smoothly. But they also move without awareness on our part, without questions, without self-consciousness.

At the other extreme from the life of habit there is the sudden break in our routine activity, the event so new and different that we are startled into noticing it. This is what it means, in Dewey's special language, to have a "sensation." It is not a mere feeling, like the feeling of being tickled or the seeing of a brown patch of color. It is to be aroused by the unusual, to have the kind of experience in which "sensational" journalism specializes. And just as an individual is passive when he is wholly a creature of habit, he is also passive when he is overcome by sensation. It is something that happens to him, that plays over him, and that he may enjoy because it releases him from routine and returns an edge to his consciousness. But he cannot do anything about it except notice it. The moment that he can fit it into his own normal pattern of life and work it ceases to be merely sensational. It becomes something he can use, grist for his intellectual mill. It stops being a "sensation" and becomes something he can make sense of.

But these extremes of routine and shock between which so

much human experience oscillates suggest what it is to have "experience" in the ideal sense. We have "an experience" when our habits are interrupted, when novelty intrudes, and when we master this novelty by developing the ideas that allow us to fit it into a new pattern of successful action. We have experiences, in short, when we solve problems. And the point of successful problem solving for Dewey is not simply that it allows us to return to the even, habitual tenor of our ways but that it provides us with those moments in which we are most intensely conscious of our surroundings, most aware of our own purposes, and most cognizant of the relation between our surroundings and our purposes. To have an experience is to have a story to tell. It is to move in an orderly way from a blocked purpose through a series of exploratory actions to a conclusion in which our purpose is realized or at least intelligibly defeated. Experience, in this sense, is its own reward. It is a means to having other experiences, but it is also—although Dewey did not like the expression—an end in itself. And in terms of this view of experience, the problematic is more interesting than what is settled, and taking risks and acting deliberately on hypotheses is to be preferred to the illusions of safety and certainty.

Dewey, it is plain, was using the word "experience" in his own way. Moreover, his theory of experience was not quite what he made it seem. Until the end of his life Dewey retained the habits of a not quite reformed philosophical idealist. He did not believe that there is a clear distinction to be made between descriptions of the facts and judgments of value, and he presented his theory of experience as though he were giving an account of the growth of experience out of habit and sensation. He admitted that human experience in fact contained many moments that were merely passages to something else and had no intrinsic worth of their own, and that there were other moments that were just dead ends. But instead of deploring these facts on explicit moral or aesthetic grounds he preferred to suggest that they were somehow instances of experience nipped in the bud, cut off before it had come to full development.

But the notion of "development" always contains an implicit standard of what is normal or desirable. We want a ten-year-old boy to grow, for example, but at some point we should also like to see him stop growing. Dewey, I believe, would have helped his readers immeasurably, and would have avoided much unnecessary controversy, if he had presented his theory of experience for what it was. It was not a psychologist's account of the laws that govern human perception or motivation, or a sociologist's account of the relation of the individual's attitudes and behavior to his culture, class, or social role. It leaned on such facts (or on guesses about such facts). But its purpose was not description for its own sake; its purpose was to describe a kind of experience that sometimes occurs and that Dewey thought ought to occur more frequently, and to show the conditions under which such experience may be blocked or realized. Facts are not irrelevant to it; but appeal to facts alone will not suffice to justify it. We also have to share Dewey's implicit ideals.

Once we adopt these ideals even provisionally, however, a new landscape opens before us. For Dewey employed his notion of ideal experience to develop a remarkably trenchant and comprehensive critique of Western philosophy and culture. The views of human experience that had prevailed in the past were not, to his mind, transcripts of unchanging truths about the human scene. They were reflections of specific social conditions, and of conditions that need no longer exist. Men had lived in a world which for the most part they could not control. So they had looked to pure reason to provide them with a refuge, and had used philosophy to paint a picture of another and better world—a "real" world behind phenomena—where everything was permanent and safe. Even more to the point, men had lived in a social world rigidly divided into separate classes. The great majority had done manual work; a tiny minority had enjoyed leisure and "culture." So the practical, the useful, the material, had been denigrated; the contemplative and the useless had been the things to admire.

In short, such conditions had created, Dewey believed, the traditional philosophical "dualisms," the sharp divisions that philosophers had characteristically set between mind and matter, reason and the senses, values and facts. In Dewey's view intelligence, when properly understood, is the activity of a biological creature, caught in mid-passage by some block to his habits or interests, and seeking and finding new habits that will be effective in place of the routines that do not work. In such a view of intelligence there is no place for separating the work of thought and the work of the senses, the movements of the mind and the effective manipulation of the physical environment. All are phases of the same activity and all support one another. In such circumstances, mind and matter, reasoning and sensing, are effectively one, and philosophical dualisms that place them in separate categories merely reinforce attitudes and habits of behavior that prevent men from having experience in its ideal form.

Once more, of course, all this raises questions. But before we turn to these questions, it is important to see what we can easily fail to see. In a sense, Dewey's ideas suffer from their very sanity: we may not recognize how fresh and radical they were. For Dewey's conception of intelligence restored men to a view of themselves that the most powerful traditions in Western philosophy and religion had tended to obscure.

If Dewey was right, then the mind is not a mysterious ghost in the machine of the body. It is simply one type of physical disposition and activity. If Dewey was right, there is no world of eternal ideas, and no order of original, pure perceptions, to which our ideas must conform. Our ideas derive their meaning from the uses we give them in specific contexts of language and inquiry. And if Dewey was right, our thinking does not normally fall into neat, military divisions marked "thinking about facts" and "thinking about values." Accordingly, moral insight is not the special prerogative of the humanities or religion or metaphysics; and if men in these fields have opinions about either facts or values, these opinions must meet the same tests that beliefs in any other field must meet.

But questions remain. There are questions, for example, about the accuracy of Dewey's account of the philosophical past, and questions, as well, about the lengths to which Dewey's fear of "dualisms" led him. To argue, for instance, that thinking about values is not independent of thinking about facts is one thing. But to say that a value judgment cannot be distinguished from a judgment about the facts is quite another. Yet this is what Dewey sometimes seems to suggest. But perhaps the greatest question raised by Dewey's theory of experience and culture, which is to say his notion of right experience and right culture, is the implicit value judgment that it involves. "Ideas are worthless," Dewey wrote, "except as they pass into actions which rearrange and reconstruct in some way, be it little or large, the world in which we live." Surely it can be agreed that a life devoted exclusively to the mental rehearsal of possibilities would be a thin and cold affair; and it can also be agreed that a society which does not use its ideas to guide its behavior will be blind or reckless in what it does. But the kind of play of the mind that is sheer play, that does not involve an irritable reaching after decisions and programs, seems to me to have a place in any calendar of the virtues that is circumspectly drawn.

No doubt Dewey did not mean to deny this value utterly. Passages certainly can be found in his books where he tries to make a place for it and emphasizes its importance in enriching experience and in bringing it the qualities of humor and compassion. But I do not think that even his stanchest defenders will say that he did not emphasize doing and acting even more, or that it was not characteristic of him to be impatient with thought for thought's sake. He spoke for men in a rising democracy, energetic, busy, committed. But a democratic culture will be richer if it can also find a place for the disengaged mind and for a kind of thinking that is not necessarily a prelude to action.

This element of distortion in Dewey's point of view seems to me to affect his views on both science and education. His most important contribution to the philosophy of science is undoubtedly his "instrumentalist" theory of ideas. Although he owed this theory in large part to Charles Peirce, he developed and applied it with an originality that was his own. Very briefly, this theory holds that an idea is an instrument by which we move from situations in which we do not know what to think or how to act to situations in which our perplexities are dispelled. Ideas are leading principles, rules which tell us what observations to make and what inferences to draw from our observations. The truth of an idea, therefore, is a matter of its effectiveness in leading to successful predictions and to actions in which our purposes are realized—in short, its effectiveness in dealing with the particular problem that it was created to solve.

The instrumentalist theory is an immensely liberating one. It explains the function of fundamental scientific ideas like the theory of the atom and tells us what we mean when we call such ideas true even though we cannot directly observe the objects whose structure they purportedly describe. And it can be used— Dewey, in fact, did use it with great success—to dispel a host of perennially disturbing problems. In moral philosophy, for example, it has traditionally been thought that we cannot rationally determine how we ought to behave unless we have some abstract definition of "good" and "right" with which to work. But Dewey argued that our moral dilemmas arise only in definite situations where individual or social interests are blocked. What we do in such circumstances is to work out some plan of action that will eliminate the specific conflict that is troubling us. And we test this plan, not by its agreement with some general definition of "the good," but by its feasibility and its consistency with other values we actually hold. Particularly when Dewey dealt with the logic of our practical judgments he exhibited, it seems to me, a shrewd, close grasp of the facts, and a stubborn resistance to traditional intellectual follies—two qualities, it must be confessed, that are not entirely usual among philosophers.

But Dewey had the defect of this virtue. As one of his early essays, "The Logic of Practical Judgment," states explicitly, he believed that scientific thinking could be made to fit the model of practical judgment. At the very least, this is an overstatement. For while it is true that many fundamental scientific ideas have an instrumental function, it is a gross simplification (as Dewey himself sometimes recognized) to say that they are tools for manipulating the environment. Their acceptance in a scientific system depends equally on purely intellectual considerations such as economy, elegance, and the possibility of connecting them with other systems. Moreover, Dewey's insistence that thinking always remakes and re-forms the materials on which it works makes it difficult to find a place for the clearly primary objective of theoretical science—namely, to understand a world whose structure does not depend on what we think or do about it. Dewey repeatedly failed to distinguish between facts as they exist and those beliefs about the facts that have the warrant of science at some particular time. But unless this distinction is kept clearly and uncompromisingly in mind we cannot explain what Dewey himself thought the hallmark of scientific thinking—its openness to correction by further evidence.

Dewey's view of science, indeed, has something a little dated about it. It seems to be the view of a man whose fundamental ideas about science had been formed before the rise of modern physics, which, for all its practical and ominous usefulness, describes a world that transcends almost all our practical and habitual expectations. When Dewey argued that "scientific method" or "scientific habits of thought" should be diffused throughout society, what did he mean by these elusive phrases? The science that played the greatest role in Dewey's thinking was biology; and what he meant by "the scientific attitude," I would suggest, was primarily the evolutionary attitude—a recognition that nothing is exempt from change, that new circumstances require new ideas and institutions, and that we should measure the worth of these ideas and institutions not in terms of allegedly eternal truths but in terms of their contribution to the control of the human environment and the satisfaction of human interests. He was right to have believed that if such an attitude could be generally diffused in a society, a remarkably liberating revolution would take place. And he would be equally right to say, as he surely would today, that some appreciation of the intellectual significance of contemporary science should be regarded as a necessity for all educated men in our society. But the view of science and scientific method which he held is not one which is likely to warn us about the extraordinary difficulty of this task.

And so we come, by a quite natural transition, to Dewey's philosophy of education. I must be brief, and I speak with the diffidence that befits any discussion either of Dewey or of education. Dewey's philosophy of education, as Sidney Hook has argued, rests on two pillars—first, a commitment to democracy and a belief that the habits developed in the classroom are as important to a student's effective participation in democracy as the facts and ideas he acquires; second, a belief that the content and methods of instruction should be governed by the best scientific knowledge available. To this certain other propositions may also be added. Teaching is effective only when the student's perspective is taken into account and only when his active interest and participation in the work of the classroom is aroused. Further, since we do not understand facts or ideas until we know how to use them, the student must be provided with facts and ideas in contexts in which he can put them to use and test them out for himself.

Any teacher can report how easy it is to forget these principles in everyday practice, and yet they may seem too obvious to constitute a significant educational philosophy. But if they do seem obvious, this is a measure of Dewey's achievement. For they were not at all obvious when he first began to write on education. In 1892, for example, Joseph Rice made a survey of American schools in thirty-six cities. He told the story of a teacher in Chicago who, after asking a question, would say, "Don't stop to think. Tell me what you know!" In New York, Rice asked a school principal whether students were allowed to turn their heads. The man replied, "Why should they look behind when the teacher is in front of them?" This is the sort of thing that Dewey was thinking about when he emphasized that teachers teach students and not only subjects, that a spirit of inquiry should animate the classroom, and that play too has its educational uses. It is grossly untrue to say that Dewey had insufficient respect for the intellectual goals of education. His philosophy was not an attempt to make the schools more frivolous. It was an attempt to return the schools to seriousness.

But Dewey, unhappily, did write vaguely. In the hands of eager disciples, his language, never an adequate instrument for the communication of ideas, has been converted into a jargon that hides them. Moreover, as Dewey himself pointed out late in life in his little book *Experience and Education,* his philosophy of education had merely been an attempt to emphasize neglected issues in education. But many of his admirers have taken a matter of emphasis for the whole story. Although I remain diffident, I cannot forbear saying that the results have frequently been bizarre.

I can mention only one issue, an issue raised by Dewey's emphasis on "the practical." It has led, I would suggest, to a mistaken conception of the kind of thing that needs to be done to involve a student actively in the learning process. Dewey was right to think that a student will master an idea only when he has had a chance to use it for himself. But it is wrong to conclude that the student can learn the use of important ideas by focusing primarily on homely problems within the round of his daily experience. If ideas have a direct bearing on such issues, that is all to the good. The alert teacher will exploit the opportunity. But we learn the distinctive function of an important idea when we see it at work, not simply reorganizing the world we have known, but leading to other worlds we might never have imagined otherwise. Accordingly, unless the student's attention to things outside his ordinary world is deliberately engaged, and unless his perceptions are liberated from domination by the familiar, the school will not have done its job.

Although Dewey would undoubtedly have agreed with this truism, I believe that he must bear some of the responsibility for the tendency of those who espouse his educational philosophy to forget it. For there is a repeated error into which Dewey falls in his educational philosophy, and in his philosophy in general. He wished passionately to show that the everyday practical experience of men could have an ideal dimension. But he slid from this idea to the quite different one that a man's—or a child's—experience must always have a practical dimension.

And yet these criticisms do not touch the heart of what John Dewey succeeded in doing. He thought that philosophy was an instrument by which a society criticizes itself, throwing off the ideas that block its development and finding the possibilities within itself that it might work to realize. He set himself to this task and performed it with a quiet, steady passion, magnanimously, imaginatively, without nostalgia for the past or regret for the comforting dogmas that had to be sacrificed. And he put his finger on the two main issues of his day—the steady growth in the importance of science and the struggle to extend democracy—and revealed their moral meaning, their possibilities for our day-to-day experience.

Dewey helped men to see that science meant something much more than an increase in their power to control their environment. He showed that science challenged inherited forms of authority and offered an alternative way by which men could stabilize their lives. And despite all his emphasis on practical manipulation and control, Dewey also showed that science represented a revolution in the human imagination, extending human horizons and making men aware of remote and unfamiliar things. So he brought science to the same test that he brought everything else—its impact on men's immediate experience; and he taught men to value science for what it could do to enhance the meanings they found in their everyday lives.

He transformed the theory of democracy in a similar way. "The one thing in the world of value," Emerson once wrote, "is the active soul." This was the central point of Dewey's theory of experience, and it is the source of his conception of democracy. Only in a society in which the lines between classes are fluid and in which men freely mingle and communicate with one another, Dewey believed, can active souls be generated everywhere. And so he saw that democracy could mean something much more than a political form. It could mean a change in the quality of a culture, an opportunity for men to experience more and to live more intensely.

Without vanity or pretentiousness, John Dewey made himself a spokesman for the best hopes of his generation. And to our generation he leaves the image of a man of unforced courage and honesty, living by choice in the mainstream of events, and yet rising above events to a coherent vision of what men might make of themselves. He helped us to see further and to move more freely. It is to him as much as to anyone that we owe what belief we have that our own place in history can be an opportunity and not a fatality.

XII

———— ⟊ ————

The Morality of Civil Disobedience

FOR SOME TIME PAST AN OLD AND TROUBLESOME PHILOSOPHICAL issue has been at the center of public events, and it is likely to remain there for some time to come. This is the question of the morality of civil disobedience. A teachers' union threatens a strike even though a state law prohibits strikes by public employees; advocates of civil rights employ mass demonstrations of disobedience to the law to advance their cause; the governor of a Southern state deliberately obstructs the enforcement of federal laws, and declares himself thoroughly within his rights in doing so. An observer can approve the motives that lead to some of these actions and disapprove others. All, nevertheless, raise the same fundamental question: Does the individual have the right—or perhaps the duty—to disobey the law when his mind, his conscience, or his religious faith tells him that the law is unjust?

The question is as old as Socrates. It has regularly propelled men into radical examination of the premises of personal morality and civic obligation and, indeed, of government itself. And it is an interesting question not only for its philosophical implications but because it has always been a painfully practical question as well, and never more so than today.

Our period in history is frequently described as "materialistic" and "conformist," an age in which governments have enormous powers to crush the bodies and anesthetize the minds of their subjects, and in which the great masses of men and women—presumably in contrast with men and women of other times—prefer to play it safe rather than raise questions of basic moral principle. It is to the point to note, however, that massive resistance to law, justified in the name of higher moral principles like "freedom," "equality," and "national independence," has been a conspicuous feature of our period, and one of its most effective techniques of social action. Millions of ordinary people with no pretensions to being either heroes or saints have employed it in India, in South Africa, in the resistance movements against the Nazis, and in the struggle for equality for Negroes in the United States.

Moreover, such massive resistance to law is by no means confined only to supremely glorious or dangerous causes; nor is it used only by revolutionaries, underdogs, or outsiders. During Prohibition, a large number of respectable, conservative Americans dutifully broke the law in defense of what they regarded as an inalienable human right. In this case, doing one's duty happened also to be agreeable and even fashionable, but this does not change the fact that many right-thinking citizens, who today condemn pacifists or integrationists for using illegal methods to advance their cause, have themselves used such methods happily and unashamedly.

When is it justified, then, for the citizen to act as his own legislator and to decide that he will or will not obey a given law?

An answer that covers all the issues this question raises cannot be given here, nor can a set of principles be proposed that will allow anyone to make automatic and infallible judgments concerning the legitimacy or illegitimacy of specific acts of civil disobedience. Such judgments require detailed knowledge of the facts of specific cases, and such knowledge is often unavailable to the outsider. Nevertheless, it is possible to indicate some of the principal issues that are raised by civil disobedience, some of the more common mistakes that are made in thinking about these issues, and, at least in outline, the approach that one man would take toward such issues.

We can begin, it seems to me, by rejecting one extreme position. This is the view that disobedience to the law can never be justified in any circumstances. To take this position is to say one of two things: either every law that exists is a just law, or a greater wrong is always done by breaking the law. The first statement is plainly false. The second is highly doubtful. If it is true, then the signers of the Declaration of Independence, and those Germans who refused to carry out Hitler's orders, committed acts of injustice.

It is possible, however, to take a much more moderate and plausible version of this position, and many quite reasonable people do. Such people concede that disobedience to the law can sometimes be legitimate and necessary under a despotic regime. They argue, however, that civil disobedience can never be justified in a democratic society, because such a society provides its members with legal instruments for the redress of their grievances.

This is one of the standard arguments that is made, often quite sincerely, against the activities of people like supporters of the Congress of Racial Equality, who set about changing laws they find objectionable by dramatically breaking them. Such groups are often condemned for risking disorder and for spreading disrespect for the law when, so it is maintained, they could accomplish their goals a great deal more fairly and patriotically by staying within the law, and confining themselves to the courts and to methods of peaceful persuasion.

Now it is perfectly true, I believe, that there is a stronger case for obedience to the law, including bad law, in a democracy than in a dictatorship. The people who must abide by the law have presumably been consulted, and they have legal channels through which to express their protests and to work for reform. One way to define democracy is to say that it is a system whose aim is to provide alternatives to civil disobedience. Nevertheless, when applied to the kind of situation faced, say, by CORE, these generalizations, it seems to me, become cruelly abstract.

The basic fallacy in the proposition that, in a democracy, civil disobedience can never be justified, is that it confuses the *ideals* or *aims* of democracy with the inevitably less than perfect accomplishments of democracy at any given moment. In accordance with democratic ideals, the laws of a democracy may give rights and powers to individuals which, in theory, enable them to work legally for the elimination of injustices. In actual fact, however, these rights and powers may be empty. The police may be hostile, the courts biased, the elections rigged—and the legal remedies available to the individual may be unavailing against these evils.

Worse still, the majority may have demonstrated, in a series of free and honest elections, that it is unwavering in its support of what the minority regards as an unspeakable evil. This is obviously the case today in many parts of the South, where the white majority is either opposed to desegregation or not so impatient to get on with it as is the Negro minority. Are we prepared to say that majorities never err? If not, there is no absolutely conclusive reason why we must invariably give the results of an election greater weight than considerations of elementary justice.

It is true, of course, that one swallow does not make a summer, and that the test of legal democratic processes is not this or that particular success or failure, but rather the general direction in which these processes move over the long run. Still, the position that violation of the law is never justifiable so long as there are legal alternatives overstates this important truth. It fails to face at least three important exceptions to it.

In the first place, dramatic disobedience to the law by a minority may be the only effective way of catching the attention or winning the support of the majority. Most classic cases of civil disobedience, from the early Christians to Gandhi and his supporters, exemplify this truth. Civil disobedience, like almost no other technique, can shame a majority and make it ask itself just how far it is willing to go, just how seriously it really is committed to defending the status quo.

Second, there is the simple but painful factor of time. If a man is holding you down on a bed of nails, it is all very well for a bystander to say that you live in a great country in which there are legal remedies for your condition, and that you ought, therefore, to be patient and wait for these remedies to take effect. But your willingness to listen to this counsel will depend, quite properly, on the nature of the injury you are suffering.

Third, it is baseless prejudice to assume that observance of the law is *always* conducive to strengthening a democratic system while disobedience to the law can never have a salutary effect. A majority's complacent acquiescence in bad laws can undermine the faith of a minority in the power of democratic methods to rectify manifest evils; yet a vigorous democracy depends on the existence of minorities holding just such a faith. Disobedience to bad laws can sometimes jolt democratic processes into motion. Which strengthens one's hope for democracy more—the behavior of the Negroes in Birmingham who broke municipal ordinances when they staged their protest marches, or the behavior of the police, using dogs and fire hoses to assert their legal authority?

Another factor should also be taken into account. In our federal system, there are often legitimate doubts concerning the legal validity, under our Constitution, of various state or local ordinances. Disobedience to these laws is in many cases simply a practical, though painful, way of testing their legality. But even where no thought of such a test is involved, there is often present a moral issue which no one can easily dodge—least of all the man whose personal dignity and self-respect are caught up in the issue. A citizen caught in a conflict between local laws and what he thinks will be upheld as the superior federal law can sometimes afford to wait until the courts have determined the issue for him. But often he cannot afford to wait, or must take a stand in order to force a decision. This is the situation of many Negro citizens in Southern states as they confront the conflict between local and federal laws.

Yet there is another side to the story. It would be a mistake to conclude from what has been said that civil disobedience is justified, provided only that it is disobedience in the name of higher principles. Strong moral conviction is not all that is required to turn breaking the law into service to society.

Civil disobedience is not simply like other acts in which men stand up courageously for their principles. It involves violation of the law. And the law can make no provision for its violation except to hold the offender liable to punishment. This is why President Kennedy was in such a delicate position at the time of the Negro demonstrations in Birmingham. He gave many signs that, as an individual, he was in sympathy with the goals of the demonstrators. As a political leader, he probably realized that these goals could not be attained without dramatic actions that crossed the line into illegality. But as Chief Executive he could not give permission or approval to such actions.

We may admire a man like Martin Luther King, who is prepared to defy the authorities in the name of a principle, and we may think that he is entirely in the right; just the same, his right to break the law cannot be officially recognized. No society, whether free or tyrannical, can give its citizens the right to break its laws: to ask it to do so is to ask it to proclaim, as a matter of law, that its laws are not laws. If anybody ever has a right to break the law, this cannot be a legal right under the law. It has to be a moral right against the law. And this moral right is not an unlimited right to disobey any law which one regards as unjust. It is a right that is hedged about, it seems to me, with important restrictions.

First of all, the exercise of this right is subject to standards of just and fair behavior. I may be correct, for example, in thinking that an ordinance against jaywalking is an unnecessary infringement of my rights. This does not make it reasonable, however, for me to organize a giant sit-down strike in the streets which holds up traffic for a week. Conformity to the concept of justice requires that there be some proportion between the importance of the end one desires to attain and the power of the means one employs to attain it.

When applied to civil disobedience, this principle constitutes a very large restriction. Civil disobedience is an effort to change the law by making it impossible to enforce the law, or by making the price of such enforcement extremely high. It is a case, as it were, of holding the legal system to ransom. It can arouse extreme passions on one side or the other, excite and provoke the unbalanced, and make disrespect for the law a commonplace and popular attitude.

Moreover, although violence may be no part of the intention of those who practice civil disobedience, the risks of violence are present, and are part of what must be taken into account when a program of civil disobedience is being contemplated. In short, civil disobedience is a grave enterprise. It may sometimes be justified, but the provocation for it has to be equally grave. Basic principles have to be at issue. The evils being combated have to be serious evils that are liable to endure unless they are fought. And there should be reasonable grounds to believe that legal methods of fighting them are likely to be insufficient by themselves.

Nor is this the only limitation on the individual's moral right to disobey the law. The most important limitation is that his cause must be a just one. It was right for General de Gaulle to disobey Marshal Pétain; it was wrong for the commanders of the French Army in Algeria, twenty years later, to disobey General de Gaulle. Similarly, if it is absolutely necessary, and if the consequences have been properly weighed, then it is right to break the law in order to eliminate inequalities based on race. But it can never be necessary, and no weighing of consequences can ever make it right, to break the law in the name of Nazi principles. In sum, the goals of those who disobey the law have to lie at the very heart of what we regard as morality before we can say that they have a moral right to do what they are doing.

But who is to make these difficult decisions? Who is to say that one man's moral principles are right and another man's wrong? We come here to the special function that civil disobedience serves in a society. The man who breaks the law on the ground that the law is immoral asks the rest of us, in effect, to trust him, or to trust those he trusts, in preference to the established conventions and authorities of our society. He has taken a large and visible chance, and implicitly asked us to join him in taking that chance, on the probity of his personal moral judgment. In doing so, he has put it to us whether we are willing to take a similar chance on the probity of our own judgment.

Thomas Hobbes, who knew the trouble that rebels and dissenters convinced of their rectitude could cause, once remarked that a man may be convinced that God has commanded him to act as he has, but that God, after all, does not command other men to believe that this is so. The man who chooses to disobey the law on grounds of principle may be a saint, but he may also be a madman. He may be a courageous and lonely individualist, but he may also merely be taking orders and following his own crowd. Whatever he may be, however, his existence tends to make us painfully aware that we too are implicitly making choices, and must bear responsibility for the ones we make.

This, indeed, may be the most important function of those who practice civil disobedience. They remind us that the man who obeys the law has as much of an obligation to look into the morality of his acts and the rationality of his society as does the man who breaks the law. The occurrence of civil disobedience can never be a happy phenomenon; when it is justified, something is seriously wrong with the society in which it takes place. But the man who puts his conscience above the law, though he may be right or he may be wrong, does take personal moral responsibility for the social arrangements under which he lives.

And so he dramatizes the fascinating and fearful possibility that those who obey the law might do the same. They might obey the law and support what exists, not out of habit or fear, but because they have freely chosen to do so, and are prepared to live with their consciences after having made that choice.

XIII

―――ᵀ――

Religion—Within Reason

RELIGION IS A PRIMORDIAL PHENOMENON ON THE HUMAN SCENE, and it has always been a troublesome one. It is not a habit of men to be reasonable about the things they care for most, and it has not been their habit to be reasonable about religion. No balanced estimate of religion's role in human history can overlook the fact that it has been a principal repository of sanctimonious foolishness and of beliefs and practices that do no credit to anything in man but his credulity and ferocity. Religions have imposed impossible demands on human flesh; they have encouraged hypocrisy and fanaticism in the human mind; they have perpetuated ideas and moral codes that have nothing to be said for them except that they rest on a revelation that lies beyond human logic and human moral sensibilities.

But religion has also been the principal teacher and comforter of mankind. It is through their religions that men have built for themselves worlds with which their hearts could make some contact—worlds in which their sense of what ultimately counts has become vivid and immediate and has found some satisfaction. Men have received from their religions an organized picture of the forces that play around human life and through it; they have received a moral estimate of these forces; they have learned about the saints and heaven and hell; they have had their minds fixed on the moral geography of this world and on the distant possibilities that lie beyond it.

> . . . my Sight, whose Sphere
> . . . Ran parallel with that of Heven here:
> It did encompass & possess Rare Things,
> But yet felt more; & on Angelic Wings
> Pierc'd throu the Skies immediatly, & sought
> For all that could beyond all worlds be thought.[1]

Religion has not been the only vehicle by which men have sought for all that could beyond all worlds be thought. In its own different way, mathematics, for example, has had the same object. But for most of its history, religion has been the principal vehicle of organized imagination available to ordinary men. It has been the shelter of the arts, the home of music, the stimulus which has lifted men's minds from seen things in front of them to unseen things beyond. When men have taken their religions seriously, and when they have also been blessed with a native irony and good sense, they have been chastened, strengthened, and released. And most of all, they have been consoled.

It is equally true to say of religion, then, that it has made this world supportable and that it has made it insupportable. And so it is natural to ask whether a line can be drawn between these two sides of religion—between the ennobling and the degrading in religion, the rational and the irrational. Is it possible to have a religion tame enough not to encourage us in our follies, but yet not so tame that it leaves us unmoved? Can religion be

[1] Thomas Traherne, *Poems of Felicity.*

brought under the governance of reason and still retain its afflatus and charm?

The question is a recurrent one. In asking it, men have wished, in the first place, to find religious beliefs that squared with the best warranted knowledge available and with the standards of responsible inquiry in other domains. And they have wished, in the second place, to keep religion within decent moral and social bounds. For whatever may be its place in the politics of eternity, religion is also a human institution that must take its place among the going affairs of men and be measured at least in part by its effects on other human activities.

Religion is hard to define, and not least because there is really no such thing as religion. There are only religions—and they do not always see eye to eye on what their main business is. Nevertheless, if we look with an anthropologist's eye at what are normally called religions, they will be seen, I believe, to have at least four aspects; and if we look at our ordinary language, we can also note at least four ways in which we normally use the words "religion" and "religious." "Religion" stands for a certain kind of psychological experience; for a creed—a set of beliefs about what are thought to be the most important facts in the universe and about the values and commitments that men should adopt in view of these facts; for a social institution in which ritual plays a large and crucial part; and, finally, for a kind of ethic, a "way of life" that seems to go beyond the conventions and necessities of practical life. Each of these elements of religion may occur in the absence of the others. But by and large, and for the mass of humanity, they come together. The health or illness of a religion usually depends on the degree to which these four aspects of its activities constitute an integrated whole.

Each of these aspects of religion is now challenged in fundamental ways in which it has not been challenged before. And it
would be well to begin an examination of these challenges by
looking at religion as a psychological phenomenon. For religion
as a personal experience is frequently a very persuasive affair. It
leads men to hold convictions on which they are prepared to do
battle with the world, convictions which they regard as immune
to criticism from any external source. It provides, therefore, a
dramatic arena for studying the interplay of religion and reason.

Since the time of William James there has been more or less
agreement about the major traits of religion considered as a
psychological phenomenon. Religious experience, in its intense
forms, seems to be a vivid sense of a truth come alive, a feeling
that things come together in a pattern that has meaning and
purpose. In religious experience men have the intuition that
the disparate parts of their lives, the scattered fragments of their
world, are somehow parts of a larger order,

> . . . blossoms upon one tree;
> Characters of the great Apocalypse,
> The types and symbols of eternity . . .

A religious experience, accordingly, is felt as a moment of
illumination and reorientation, a way of seeing things as they
have not been seen before. Our ordinary habits are arrested, our
conventional world is shaken up, the pieces of the puzzle finally
come together. Having had this experience, we have the feeling
that the world exists on two levels, one really real, the other not
so real. We have the feeling that we can see *through* things—
through the dross and vanity of our ordinary affairs—to what
they invisibly but really mean. With this feeling there goes the

sense of having a new power that is not quite one's own and of being actively committed to something more enduring and important than one's own personal interests and ambitions. The religious man is lifted out of himself. He may be lifted out of himself to such an extent that he feels not merely bound to what is outside him but wholly at one with it. He has found his proper element; and as he bathes in it, the old distinction between subject and object disappears.

Clearly, the experience is an impressive one for those who have had it. It is impressive enough from any point of view to suggest two questions. The first is a question of fact: What is the state of religious feeling today, and where do we find it?

The answer cannot be encouraging, I suspect, to anyone concerned about the future of organized religion—or, at any rate, concerned about more than its external forms. To find examples in the past of the kind of experience I have described one would go to the classic literature of the saints and mystics— Saint Paul, Saint Augustine, Pascal, Jakob Boehme. To find examples of this sort of experience today one goes to the literature of secular politics. Some fresh and touching examples of religious feeling can, of course, be found on the contemporary scene within the traditional setting of our inherited religions. But for the most part the religious feeling that seems to be making the difference and moving the world is the feeling that has been aroused by the abstractions and symbols of an era of ideologies. A release from the dark night of the soul, a sense of comradeship in the service of a higher cause, an answer to the desire to find a coherence and pattern in the world—these are what our ideologies offer.

Much current discussion of the decline of religious feeling in the modern world seems to me beside the point. For the present century is a period of religious feeling which is perhaps as wide-spread, and at least as intense, as can be found in any of the so-called "Ages of Belief." Similarly, the rise, real or alleged, in church attendance seems to me equally irrelevant in judging the present state of our inherited religions, or in guessing their future. For it is the language of secular ideologies that one hears in most churches. In short, whether inside the churches or outside the churches, the challenge to inherited religion is the same: it is that religious emotions have shifted from their traditional objects.

But there is still a second question to ask. It is a question of principle. What place should religious experience have, what credit should we give it, in forming our ultimate beliefs? Are the conclusions to which a religious experience may lead us subject to the same tests that any other beliefs must meet? Or do they stand in a world of their own, immune to criticism from the outside?

There is a puzzling feature of what we have called religious experience, and it has led at least some to think twice about what is meant by "reason." Religious feeling is an externalized feeling, a feeling directed outward from the self. And yet, curiously enough, it does not seem to have a clear and definite object. Money, an ikon, a Beatrice, the memory of Christ crucified—in one sense, all these are objects of religious emotion. But to the extent that they are objects of *religious* emotion their enchantment does not in the end seem to be their own. Religious feelings move toward them and then through them toward what they symbolize—and what they symbolize cannot apparently be seen in any ordinary sense or described in any ordinary way. The ultimate object of religious worship cannot be easily located in time or space; the more we pursue it the more it eludes our grasp; in the ordinary sense, it is not really an object at all. Attempt to state clearly and definitely what it is that you feel religious about, and it is likely to seem trite, or foolish, or sentimental. Even more likely, you will fail in being more than vague. We usually describe God, it should be noticed, by announcing what He is not. The natural language of religion seems to be parable and paradox.

Thus it is that discussions of the relation of religion to reason can be so unsatisfactory. The partisans of reason and the partisans of religion pass each other like ships in the night. The partisan of reason would like to know what it is that the religious believer asserts as the result of having had a religious experience; and he would like to take that assertion and determine whether it is true or false, probable or improbable, in accordance with the standards he employs for criticizing other beliefs. On the other hand, the man who has had a religious experience, and who has been moved to hold certain conclusions as a result, is convinced that any attempt to pin down religious assertions by such rules is to miss their very essence. Religious belief, he is convinced, has a status of its own. To hold a religious belief is not like holding any other kind of belief. Therefore it cannot be examined in the way we examine other kinds of belief, or be judged by the same standards.

This position can be stated in the language of current philosophy. It has been said by some recent philosophers that to seek to judge religious beliefs in the light of their truth, and to mean by truth the same thing that we mean in other domains, is to commit a peculiarly awful kind of mistake—what is called a "category mistake." Consider, for example, the case of a man who says of a lady, "She wears her grief like a new spring dress." Imagine his plight if he heard this statement rejected as false by some unimaginative listener, and on the ground that no one can wear grief because it has no sleeves or other physical properties. Yet the partisan of reason, it is asserted, is just as unimaginative as this with regard to religion. He fails to see that religious language arises in response to the unusual sort of experience that religion represents. It has the task of conveying what cannot quite be conveyed in words, of talking about events and objects that are not like ordinary events and objects. So religion has to use words in a stretched and unusual way; it has its own inner logic; and it is a radical mistake, as well as evidence of a lack of imagination, to judge it by any logic but its own.

This position, as you will recognize, is not a wholly new one. But it has recently come forward again dressed (I use the word in its religious or stretched sense) in the costume of current and highly creditable styles in philosophy. In this form it has found favor among an increasing number of contemporary philosophers and theologians. I must confess, however, that I remain unpersuaded. In explaining why I am unpersuaded, I come to the question of religion as a creed. Can the claim be sustained that religion provides a special avenue to truth? Does it give us valid insights into the nature of the universe and of man's place and purpose within it which we could not acquire in any other way, and which we cannot criticize from any external point of view?

The assertion that religious beliefs occupy a world that is wholly their own seems to me indefensible on a number of grounds. For one thing, it does not help us to choose among religions—which, after all, have a number of quite different things to say about the world. For another, it isolates religion from everything else—which is the last thing that anyone would think that a lover of religion would wish to do. But I shall dwell on two other considerations—namely, that this position is overly enthusiastic in its estimate of how unusual religious experience is and that it is artificial in its characterization of religious belief.

Let me ask, first, how unusual religious experience is. I do not mean whether religious experiences are frequent. I mean whether, when they do occur, they exhibit characteristics so special that it is legitimate to develop a brand-new department of logic to take care of them. This does not seem to me to be the case. For it is not only so-called religious experiences that leave us with the belief that words can never wholly capture what is sensed or felt. Take any object or event that is not wholly novel, or that is not so routine that you do not pay genuine attention to it: it comes soaked in associations and meanings. If we should try to track down and state all these associations, we should never succeed. It should be no surprise that words are not substitutes for concrete experiences, or that something of what we feel or sense will always pass through the net of language. This is as true in every other domain as in religion. And it should neither be deplored nor converted into an argument for the supreme truth of the unutterable. For it is precisely because language is not identical with that which it expresses or describes that we can use it to formulate true statements about selected features of our experience.

To use it in this way, however, we have to use it in accordance with certain rules: among other things, we have to delimit the area of our attention, to assign stable meanings to our words, to use them with precision and consistency. If religious language cannot be used in this way, it can only be because those who use it do not wish to do so—and this means that they are not using language in the way it has to be used if beliefs capable of being called true or false are to be formulated.

There is no reason, of course, why language must always be used in this way, and many reasons why it should not. Language has other purposes, including the expression of religious emotions, which are as important as inquiry after truth. But when language is not used in a way that is appropriate for inquiry after truth, then we should not claim the value of truth for what it says. We cannot have our cake and eat it too. We cannot say that religious beliefs deal with the unutterable and then claim that they are true.

But the argument that "religious truth" is a special kind of truth seems to me to be questionable on much simpler grounds. It seems to me to falsify the actual way in which most people hold their religious beliefs. It is true that there is an aura of ineffable mystery about many—perhaps most—traditional religious beliefs. But at least some of these doctrines assert the occurrence of specific historical events, or the existence of certain facts or laws. When the believer says that these doctrines are true, he means, unless I am gravely mistaken, that they are true in a quite ordinary sense of the word. He may accept the story of the Exodus from Egypt, for example, and care about it, and take it to his heart, because of all that it represents—the age-old sufferings of his people, the strength their faith has given them, the transcendent significance of freedom. But if he believes that it is true, he believes also that it actually happened—that if he had been present at the right time and place he would have seen quite real individuals fleeing from slavery in Egypt. If this is not the case, it would be difficult to explain why so many who have held religious beliefs have been disturbed when they have come across historical or other findings that seem to challenge what they believe. Philosophical or theological arguments which inform them that they ought not to be disturbed—that, indeed, they are committing a "category mistake" when they are disturbed—seem to be saving religious belief at the price of discarding what most people mean when they say they believe in one or another of the traditional religions.

The point, elementary though it may be, is worth emphasizing because much has recently been said about the "poetic" or "symbolic" truth of religion. The great religions, it need hardly be said, are storehouses of stories and traditions that are symbols and archetypes of recurrent human experiences. One can read out of these stories generalizations about the human scene that are plainly true—though it should be added that not all of them are. But if we accept a religion on these grounds, we accept it on the same grounds on which we might accept, say, Goethe's *Faust* as true. So we give up precisely the claim which, in most people's minds, distinguishes the stories of religion from other stories—namely, that they are not merely "symbolically" true, but true without a qualifying adjective.

I should add that it seems to me not impossible that a religion could draw the genuine and passionate adherence of its members while it claimed nothing more than to be a poetry in which men might participate and from which they might draw strength and light. The special power of religious stories, their difference from Goethe's *Faust,* lies in the fact that men through the ages have participated in them, that they have no individual author but come to us as collective products, drenched in the sufferings and hopes of our ancestors. I suspect that it is this symbolic and imaginative power of religion that has in fact drawn many of its adherents in the past. And a rational religion, claiming no special revelation and no absolute validity for all men, and admitting that its stories were legends and its gods simply personifications of human ideals, would not necessarily be less moving than the traditional religions of the past. It would only be less demanding of intellectual sacrifices. But to proceed on this path such a religion would have to say what few religions, past and present, have been willing to say— that religion can make no claim to a special insight into truth. It can claim only to speak the truth in a peculiarly arresting and beautiful way—and this only sometimes.

Could such a religion succeed? I believe that it could—provided only that it spoke always with the tongues of angels.

This brings me to religion as ritual. The religious emotion is different from other emotions of illumination and reorientation because it is usually the result of a specific performance. The poetry of religion is different from other poetry because it is a poetry in which men act together. Religion, in short, is a social ritual. It turns around certain regular, disciplined performances, which are repeated on specified occasions. They are practiced by men together; and they normally serve to give men a sense of closer community with each other. For the power of a ritual derives from the fact that it symbolizes things beyond itself, things of peculiar and inescapable importance.

Voltaire once remarked that religion would never die because there would always be people who liked to sing and drink on Saturday evening and wished to continue on Sunday morning. Unless one has an unreasoning prejudice against singing and drinking, the remark does not so much deflate religion as explain it. Over the long pull men have not gone to church only, or even mainly, out of a sense of duty, or as the result of having been nagged into it, or even because they thought it helped them remain, or seem, respectable. They have gone because churches were beautiful, because their friends were there, because music and dancing and bread and wine are naturally delightful—and doubly so when they stand for those things on which a man believes that his whole fate turns. The dangers of ritual are notorious—its hypnotic effects, its support of outworn traditions and used-up ideals, its suppression of spontaneity, its tendency to degenerate into an empty form. But these dangers are not inevitable to ritual. When a ritual is attached to beliefs that we think are true, and when the ideals it portrays have an appeal of their own, it is the social instrument by which ordinary things become extraordinary, and the everyday currency of our lives takes on ideal meanings.

The decline of an effective ritual in contemporary religions seems to me no less important in estimating their future than their decline in intellectual substance. In part, the appeal of religious ritual has declined because men can find their entertainment elsewhere. In part it has declined because it has become increasingly abstract. Historically, the church in most communities was the home of a wide variety of activities. It was the center for charity, for education, for news, for gossip, for organizing collective action and exerting political pressure. Rituals practiced under such conditions came suffused with the memories and emotions of a common life. Religious rituals today, unhappily, have less to lean on and less of an immediate and pressing nature to do.

But there is also another reason, I suspect, for the decline of an effective religious ritual. It emerges in part when we reflect on the obvious fact that the rituals of the religions we inherit generally symbolize the experience of agrarian peoples while we are living in a mainly urban and suburban civilization. This obvious fact has a deeper implication. The rituals of the major religions have characteristically symbolized the great inescapable facts of human destiny, and facts immediately present to everyone's view—birth, sex, the cycle of the seasons, death. But while these remain inescapable facts of our destiny, they are for us less and less everyday facts with which we live. They are rumors and reports, things we seal off in hospital rooms or have to learn about initially by hearsay. I hope that I shall not be misunderstood: I am not proposing that we return to dying in the streets because it will have educational effects on our children. I mean only that those of us who grow up or live out our lives in the modern city and suburb see few things that have not been made by man. And so, for all our abstract knowledge of the ways of the world, it is hard to take home to our hearts the truth that the rituals of the great religions celebrate—that, in the end, man does not live in a world he has made for himself.

I come in this way to my final theme—religion considered as a distinctive ethic, and religion in its relation to ethics. I want to make a modest case for a point that I think is unduly neglected; and I may introduce it best, I think, by a brief observation about the currently popular dictum that the world's ills would be cured if only we lived up to our religions. This dictum seems to me to propose a policy that is not only impossible but would be the cause of considerable trouble if it were possible. It is the believer in Sean O'Casey's *The Plough and the Stars* who replies indignantly to the blasphemies of an unbeliever: "There's no reason to bring religion into it. I think we ought to have as great a regard for religion as we can, so as to keep it out of as many things as possible."

It is easy to forget that the religions of the world have not always come to make the world more comfortable, but at least sometimes, if their leading apostles can be believed, to make it more uncomfortable. For it must simply be faced that religions have a habit of making extreme claims on their adherents. A man seriously committed to a religious faith has much more than what now passes in many quarters for religion—that is, a bland sense of good-fellowship together with a pleasant conviction that he belongs to the same club the universe belongs to. A man who is serious about his religion is likely to feel that his life depends upon it. If he believes that his religion deals with the things of another world, he may view everything in this world as a contamination and a curse—in which case he is likely to quarantine himself. If he believes that his religion has come to make the world over, he may feel that it is involved everywhere—in which case he will find it difficult to make any compromises. Both these attitudes may be admirable, but neither makes for decent living conditions.

It is the barest truism to say that in our ordinary affairs we employ moral standards, and must employ moral standards, that are not wholly compatible with what our religions, taken uncompromisingly, demand of us. Few things could be more attractive, for example, than the vision of Saint Francis' comradeship with the beasts of the field. But few things would be more inconvenient than the conversion of Saint Francis' example into a general social policy. Some may take this as a proof of original sin. I confess that I accept it with a measure of relief.

Nor is it only the secular-minded who are anxious that we keep our religious propensities within bounds. Most of those who have been responsible for the practical administration of religious groups also have made it plain that while there is a religious morality proper to saints, there is also a compromise more appropriate for ordinary men. "The unmarried man," wrote Saint Paul, "is anxious about the Lord's affairs, how best to satisfy the Lord; the married man is anxious about worldly affairs, how best to satisfy his wife—so he is torn in two directions." But Saint Paul accepted the necessity of compromise in most cases: "There is so much immorality that every man had better have a wife of his own and every woman a husband of her own. . . . But what I have just said is by way of concession, not command."[2]

But the limitations of transcendental religion—of religion as the worship of perfections, however conceived—also suggests something of what religion has done, and might still do. It is usual in current discussions of the relation of religion to morals to focus on the relations of religion to practical morality, to the morality of concrete achievement. It does not seem to me that religion is either necessary or sufficient to a moral life in this secular and worldly sense—although, despite what I have said about the dangers of religious fanaticism and otherworldliness, religion need not be incompatible with, and can obviously sometimes help, the secular moral life. But all this leaves out what may well be the distinctive contribution that an emancipated religion might make to morality.

Religion has frequently meant a morality with a special flavor, a special angle of vision on any morality. It might still mean, as it has sometimes meant in the past, this morality of transcendence: the attitude that comes from looking beyond even human ideals and the human effort to realize them—the willing commitment to what lies beyond human powers to change.

No unusual or occult vision is needed to produce this attitude, and the conclusions to which it leads need neither offend our common sense nor cause us to withdraw from the ordinary

2 I Corinthians.

concerns of men. At the conclusion of the *Iliad* there is an experience which produces such an attitude, and it comes, in the midst of a foolish and brutal war, to Priam, a king and patriot, and to Achilles, the sulky, impulsive, and bullying warrior. Priam, the father of the slain Hector, comes to Achilles to beg for the return of his son's body:

"Think of your father [says Priam], who is such even as I am, on the sad threshold of old age. . . . Think on your own father and have compassion upon me, who am the more pitiable, for I have steeled myself as no man has ever yet steeled himself before me, and have raised to my lips the hand of him who slew my son."

Thus spoke Priam, and the heart of Achilles yearned as he bethought him of his father. He took the old man's hand and moved him gently away. The two wept bitterly—Priam . . . weeping for Hector, and Achilles, now for his father and now for Patroclus, till the house was filled with their lamentation. But when Achilles was now sated with grief and had unburdened the bitterness of his sorrow, he left his seat and raised the old man by the hand. . . . Then he said: "Unhappy man, you have indeed been greatly daring. . . . Sit now upon this seat, and for all our grief we will hide our sorrows in our hearts, for weeping will not avail us. The immortals know no care, yet the lot they spin for man is full of sorrow. . . . Even so did it befall Peleus; the gods endowed him with all good things from his birth upwards. . . . But even on him, too, did heaven send misfortune, for there is no race of royal children born to him in his house, save one son who is doomed to die all untimely; nor may I take care of him now that he is growing old, for I must stay here at Troy to be the bane of you and your children.

"And you too, O Priam, I have heard that you were aforetime happy. . . . But from the day when the dwellers in heaven sent this evil upon you, war and slaughter have been about your city continually. Bear up against it, and let there be some intervals in your sorrow. Mourn as you may for your brave son, you will take nothing by it. You cannot raise him from the dead; ere you do so yet another sorrow shall befall you."

Then Achilles has Hector's body washed and anointed, and places it upon a bier to be returned to Priam.

"Sir," he said, "your son is now laid upon his bier and is ransomed according to your desire. You shall look upon him when you take him away at daybreak; for the present let us prepare our supper."[3]

It is proper that the *Iliad* ends here, with this recognition by its principal actors of their common sorrow and helplessness. For while the war will go on, it cannot have the same meaning for either side afterwards.

Such an experience has neither magic nor mystery about it. But it is not different from what, in religious language, is called "transfiguration." Those who have it are illuminated and re-oriented. They are, at least for the moment, taken out of themselves and brought before larger and more enduring things, things they cannot change. And yet these men themselves are changed—and changed, singularly enough, from passive sufferers to active agents. They regain the initiative. Even though they may be in the grip of an inexorable fate, they are not overwhelmed by events. They do what they have to do; and they do it out of an active decision that it must be done. "Let us prepare our supper," says Achilles. "You can weep for your dear son hereafter." "Come, get up and let us go," says Jesus. "Here is my betrayer close at hand."

Such an attitude—the attitude that comes from looking occasionally at the unchanging and unmoved sky—is not an easy one. But it seems to me a main source from which we might

3 Samuel Butler translation.

draw resolution, powers of endurance, and charity. We might draw from it, too, something else about which much is said these days—a tragic sense of life—and something else intimately connected with it—a sense of proportion, a sense of humor. For neither tragedy nor comedy can exist except as we recognize the gap between our high images of our destiny and what in fact we are. There is humility in such an attitude, but there is a triumph over meanness in it, too. It is the only sure triumph over our condition that we mortal beings can have.

Those who truly love God, said Spinoza, cannot expect that God will love them in return. Most religions in the past, and most today, have not encouraged such an attitude, but rather its reverse. They have fed us on sweets. But I cannot help but think that in their best moments it has been this message of deliverance from our vanity and from the vanity of things, of willing commitment to the necessities that are not of our making, that has been at their heart.

Acknowledgments

"Existentialism, or Cosmic Hypochondria" is a revised version of two essays that first appeared in *The Saturday Review*.

"The Family in Context" was delivered as a keynote address before the National Conference on Social Welfare, and was subsequently published in the proceedings of the Conference, *Helping the Family in Urban Society,* ed. by Fred DelliQuadri, Columbia University Press, 1963.

"The Barges on the Seine" was first published in *Harper's Magazine*.

"The Love of Anxiety" was delivered as the Annie Talbot Cole Lecture at Bowdoin College in 1963.

"The Bear and the Beaver" was first published by William Sloane Associates.

"The Awful Idea of Being an Individual" was a convocation address delivered at the Centennial celebration of the University of Denver in 1964, devoted to the theme of the nature, rights, and responsibilities of the individual.

"George Santayana: Solitude and Sincerity in Philosophy" is based on two essays, one of which appeared in *The Saturday Review* and the other in the *New York Times Book Review*.

"Four Illusions of Foreign Policy," and "The Morality of Civil Disobedience," appeared in the *New York Times Magazine*.

"John Dewey's Legacy" was delivered as part of the ceremonies at The Johns Hopkins University in 1959 commemorating the hundredth anniversary of Dewey's birth. It was subsequently published in *The American Scholar*.

"Religion—Within Reason" was delivered as the Ware Lecture to the American Unitarian Association in 1957.

I am grateful to the publishers, periodicals, and institutions named for permission to reprint these pieces here. Most of the essays have been slightly revised, and some fairly extensively. In a number of cases I have also substituted a new title for the one under which the essay originally appeared.

C.F.

ABOUT THE AUTHOR

Charles Frankel was born in New York City and educated at Columbia and Cornell. He has been a member of the Department of Philosophy at Columbia since 1939, except for the war years, when he was on active duty with the Navy as a Japanese language specialist particularly concerned with military government. He has won academic distinctions, including a Guggenheim Fellowship and a Carnegie Corporation "Reflective Year" Fellowship, but his activities have been varied, ranging from the conduct of the CBS-TV program, "The World of Ideas," to being the principal author of the Rockefeller Panel Report on American Democracy, "The Power of the Democratic Idea." His writing for periodicals has also covered a broad spectrum, from the technical learned journals to *Harper's Magazine, The New Yorker,* and *The New York Times Magazine.* Professor Frankel's books include *The Case for Modern Man, The Golden Age of American Philosophy, The Democratic Prospect,* and *The Love of Anxiety.*

Format by Katharine Sitterly
Set in Linotype Baskerville
Composed, printed and bound by American Book–Stratford Press
HARPER & ROW, PUBLISHERS, INCORPORATED